PRAISE FOR
Planting the Heavens

Apostle Tim Sheets has breathed fresh life on timeless truths. The word of faith and seed faith teachings from years ago have been joined with new revelatory teaching and married to present-day truth. The Ekklesia has been given amazing, updated weapons in order to accomplish her mission. I believe this book will activate believers to pick up their swords and fight to accomplish God's plan and purpose for the earth in this generation.

WOODIE FULTZ
Pastor, Valley Worship Center
Dayton, Ohio

Tim Sheets' masterful work, *Planting the Heavens*, will revolutionize how you think, speak, and pray. You will be inspired by the fresh revelation, encouraged by the powerful testimonies, and empowered to go out and change your world with the words you speak.

APOSTLE JANE HAMON
Vision Church at Christian International

Of all the things our omnipotent God could have done to create, He made everything in the universe—by talking! With *Planting the Heavens*, Apostle Tim Sheets reveals the effectiveness available to us when we use our words as seeds. Reading this, I have gone from conviction for not stewarding this ability to elation over the possibility. This is a real life- and Kingdom-changer.

TIM HALE
Pastor, Harbor Christian Fellowship
Lebanon, Ohio

Out of the treasury of revelations from God the Holy Spirit come the writings of a scholarly apostle who walks amongst us, Dr. Tim Sheets. Like a holy scribe, Dr. Sheets demonstrates in words God our Father's command—that His sons and daughters speak His words and His only—creating a planting into the heavens and into God's Kingdom in the earth and bringing forth some of the greatest events and changes in the lives of the people of the congregations in the cities of the nations. For the honoring of God our Father's plans and purposes in our lives, such a book, *Planting the Heavens*, now comes forth.

Dr. Mary Frances Varallo
Author, *Dare to Declare*
President, Mary Frances Varallo Ministries
Nashville, Tennessee

I know of no greater student and teacher of the Word than Dr. Tim Sheets. None. This is demonstrated in every message he preaches and every book he writes. After reading *Planting the Heavens*, you will agree. Get ready to receive much revelation from these pages!

Dutch Sheets
Author, Apostle
Dutch Sheets Ministries
Colorado Springs, Colorado

Too many believers live far beneath their potential! God has empowered His children with His very own spiritual DNA. He destined them to overcome every hindrance that blocks the blessings of the Lord. These believers have the potential to rule over sickness, poverty, injustice, and any other attack of the enemy.

Tim Sheets' very powerful and timely book, *Planting the Heavens*, provides keys to help believers shift to a new level of overcoming through the power of words. He releases revelation that unlocks supernatural faith. You will be strengthened and encouraged to use your voice to see the will of God released in the earth. I highly recommend

Planting the Heavens to anyone desiring to call forth the will of God as His change agents!

BARBARA WENTROBLE
President, International Breakthrough Ministries
President, Breakthrough Business Leaders
Author of nine books including
Prophetic Intercession, Praying with Authority, Fighting for Your Prophetic Promises, Empowered for Your Purpose

I personally owe a great debt to Dr. Tim Sheets. His books have transformed my personal prayer life and my foundational theology about "spirit led" prayer. I will never forget being at a prayer meeting in Columbus, Ohio with him that was charged with the presence of God and the power of the Holy Spirit. We not only touched heaven, we also changed the destiny of our nation in that one meeting. As a result of that prayer meeting, I know that this generation's prayer warriors can truly move mountains.

Not only is Dr. Sheets one of the nation's most anointed spiritual leaders, for years he has labored on the cutting edge of the realms of intercessory prayer and national transformation. He and his affiliated prayer warriors are responsible for creating spiritual, political, and economic change in his native state of Ohio. Don't miss the opportunity to glean from his years of dynamic prayer excursions and spiritual adventures. This work will revolutionize your understanding of the ways of God and the work of prayer.

HARRY R. JACKSON, JR.
Senior Pastor, Hope Christian Church
Bishop, International Communion of Evangelical Churches

It has been my pleasure to know Dr. Tim and Carol Sheets for the last 32 years. It has been my joy to work closely with them as a staff pastor and to be part of the first church planted from the dream that God gave to Dr. Sheets. I have been a personal witness of some of the miraculous stories written in this book and can tell you that Dr. Sheets has lived this message as long as I have known him.

There has never been a better time in the history of the nation to release this much-needed book. The nation has never been more assaulted by a war of words than in recent history. Negative words and pessimistic views have littered the landscape of the country until it has felt more like the "Divided State" than the United States. This new book will truly inspire you to treat your words with honor and with great expectations. Hebrews 3:1 calls Jesus Christ the "apostle and High Priest of our confession." This book will admonish us to come into agreement with our heavenly Father and release the life of God as a dynamic force in the earth.

DR. PATRICK MURRAY
Senior Pastor, The Living Word Church
Vandalia, Ohio

PLANTING THE
HEAVENS

DESTINY IMAGE BOOKS BY TIM SHEETS

Angel Armies

Heaven Made Real

PLANTING THE
HEAVENS

Releasing the Authority of the Kingdom Through Your
WORDS, PRAYERS, & DECLARATIONS

TIM SHEETS

DESTINY IMAGE® PUBLISHERS, INC.

P.O. Box 310, Shippensburg, PA 17257-0310

"Promoting Inspired Lives."

This book and all other Destiny Image and Destiny Image Fiction books are available at Christian bookstores and distributors worldwide.

Cover design by Eileen Rockwell
Interior design by Terry Clifton

For more information on foreign distributors, call 717-532-3040.

Reach us on the Internet: www.destinyimage.com.

ISBN 13 TP: 978-0-7684-1203-1
ISBN 13 eBook: 978-0-7684-1204-8
ISBN 13 HC: 978-0-7684-1554-4
ISBN 13 LP: 978-0-7684-1555-1

For Worldwide Distribution, Printed in the U.S.A.
1 2 3 4 5 6 7 8 / 21 20 19 18 17

And then there were six.
Madeline Hope, Lily Mei Mei, Jude Richison, Jaidin Song,
Joelle Charlotte, and Samuel Josiah.
Six precious grandchildren, pieces of my heart with destiny and
purpose, and six great reasons to plant the heavens daily.
I dedicate this book to them.

May their hope and trust always be in Him.

ACKNOWLEDGMENTS

There were countless hours of dedicated help to complete this book. My wife, Carol; our daughter, Rachel Sheets Shafer; my sister-in-law, Marie Fox; and my assistant, Katelyn Cundiff transcribed, researched, edited, proofed, read out loud over and over and over again, laughed, ate donuts, and drank endless cups of coffee in order to bring this to completion.

To the Oasis Intercessors who joined me every Wednesday night for at least six months to pray for clarity and flow to be released in printed form, I thank you. You are the Remnant without whom we could not accomplish anything.

Most of all, thank You, Lord Jesus, for Your Word, and for giving me ears to hear You. May I always represent You well.

CONTENTS

FOREWORD

This book is a battle cry and rally call to God's people. It is a source of infusion of courage necessary to change our world! We are living in unprecedented times in today's world. It would seem in the natural that things are out of control and spinning into a chaotic state. This seems to be occurring on a national and international scene. It also seems that many individuals on a personal level are in this same place of chaos. Individual dreams seem to be shattered. Families are struggling with no peace and harmony in the ranks. Financial ruin for many seems to be looming on the horizon. Sickness and disease are dominating lives with seemingly no answer available. In his book *Planting the Heavens*, Tim Sheets gives us God's strategy and answer. He addresses the bold place we as God's people are to take. As we position ourselves and begin to Plant the Heavens with God's word and power, we can see things change.

When God was ready to change the culture and climate of anything, He began by positioning a prophetic voice. When I speak of a prophetic voice, I am not talking of just a prophet. All of us are to use the prophetic unction the Holy Spirit provides us with. When we speak from this prophetic unction, it has the power to change climates and cultures. This is what happened in Ezekiel chapter 37 and verses 1 and 3.

> The hand of the LORD came upon me and brought me out in the Spirit of the LORD, and set me down in the midst of the valley; and it was full of bones. Then He caused me to pass by them all around, and behold, there were very many in the open valley; and indeed they were very dry. And He said to me, "Son of man, can these bones live?"…So I answered, "O Lord GOD, You know."

There was death and despair within a nation. God's answer was to position Ezekiel in the midst of it. We must understand that it is impossible to be placed in such an arena and not feel the pull of that depression, despair, and disillusionment. As a result, when God asked his prophet can these bones live, he responded with, "God, only you know." This was probably not the response of faith God wanted, yet the prophet was being real. God's solution was to command the prophet to prophesy to these dead and dry bones. At this point the prophet had to decide: Would he prophesy what his eyes were seeing, which was death and hopelessness? Or would he prophesy what his ears were hearing in the spirit, which was the sound of a marching, conquering army? Whatever he prophesied would determine the future of a nation!

Of course Ezekiel chose to agree with the sound of the marching and conquering army. This was, in fact, what occurred. In the times to come, Israel would be restored as a nation. They would leave the captivity they were in and would begin to live again. Ezekiel's ability and willingness to speak a word in the midst of the present hopelessness was essential to restoration. A nation's destiny was reset because a prophetic person was willing to speak the word of the Lord. The earth then lined up with the sound of this word.

I am excited about this book you hold in your hand. God is looking for some Ezekiels that He can position in some valleys of dry bones. You may wonder why you are in the place you are. It is because God has strategically placed you there to change it. God needs you. Despair, hopelessness, and shame must be shaken off. We are to take our place in the spirit and shift things into divine order and fruitfulness. We are God's answer to places of weeping. If enough people full of faith and God's prophetic unction can boldly take their place in the spirit, nations can change. Not only will people's individual lives experience the breakthrough of God, cultures will shift into their divine order. The Lord needs us to Plant the Heavens. Let's take our place in the creative agenda of God and watch lives and nations change. The heavens await our decrees, proclamations, and announcements.

ROBERT HENDERSON
Bestselling author of *Operating in the Courts of Heaven*

WORDS ARE SEEDS

Words are seeds.

I was reading Genesis 1—the awesome description of God creating the heavens and the earth. Suddenly, I heard the voice of Holy Spirit so clearly. *Words are seeds.* His voice was heavy with meaning, with *instruction*.

How many times had I read Genesis 1, penned by Moses 3,400 years ago? Countless times. But this time I leaned back from my desk, echoing aloud what was recorded in ancient history thousands of years ago. I knew Holy Spirit was giving me a truth that is still alive, still powerful, and still needs to be loosed. It was a moment of enlightenment, and I would never be the same after that revelation.

Words are seeds. "Word seeds" germinate and they grow. "Word seeds," planted properly, reproduce themselves. "Word seeds" are the concealed beginnings of something that can grow to fullness when we believe and act upon them. They are latent potential, waiting to be planted in the soil of an individual, a church, a business, or a nation that can grow and fulfill that "word seed."

We are told that God planted the heavens and the earth with word seeds—words that became what He decreed. Heaven and earth became what He seeded, decreed, and described with His words. From the beginning God was sharing with man, who was made in His image and likeness, how they could partner with Him and be creators by decreeing word seeds. We do not create from nothing like God did, but we take what God has done and steward it in such a way that we can decree a creative force into the heavens and the earth.

We can also create gardens like Eden, filled with fruit and abundance—gardens in the natural realm and the spirit realm. We can plant words filled with life—words that when believed, decreed, and acted upon become the very thing they describe. Word seeds have the innate ability to become what they are describing. They are seeds releasing their inner codes to reproduce in the soil in which they are planted.

What possibilities has God given to man? What opportunities has He given us when we understand the principle that words are seeds? Plant words of life. Plant them in the heavens. Plant them on the earth. Plant them in your life, business, and children. Plant purpose-filled seeds.

THE POWER OF OUR WORDS

Then God said, "Let the land sprout with vegetation— every sort of seed-bearing plant, and trees that grow seed-bearing fruit. These seeds will then produce the kinds of plants and trees from which they came." And that is what happened. The land produced vegetation—all sorts of seed-bearing plants, and trees with seed-bearing fruit. Their seeds produced plants and trees of the same kind. And God saw that it was good (Genesis 1:11-12 NLT).

And God said, Let the earth cause grass to spring up, herb producing seed, fruit-trees yielding fruit after their kind, the seed of which is in them, on the earth. And it was so. And the earth brought forth grass, herb producing seed after its kind, and trees yielding fruit, the seed of which is in them, after their kind. And God saw that it was good (Genesis 1:11-12 DARBY).

Words are very powerful. They effect change. They loose power. They release potential. They instruct. They release strategies that can be acted upon. God shows from the very beginning the vital importance and power of words. Nothing activates the Kingdom of God and the angel armies like the Word of God. Holy Spirit hovers until He hears the Word of God. God's Word activates His power and Kingdom resources.

Psalms 103:20 says that *angels hearken* to the voice of God's Word. The entire universe is made to respond to the voice of God's Word. The heavens and the earth are made to respond to the powerful voice of His Word. Amazingly, human beings made in His image and in His likeness are carriers of that Word when they are activated at the new birth. They are "lifed" by it when they are born again.

God's Word also opens creative spheres, releasing creativity and creative abilities. Genesis 1:2 (NKJV) says, *"The earth was without form, and void; and darkness was upon the face of the deep. And the Spirit of God was hovering over the face of the waters."* The earth was without shape, in utter chaos, and it was nonproductive. It was a barren place until God's Word came forth. Notice that the condition of the heavens and the earth were dependent on the Word of God. Its productivity was dependent on the Word of God, and it still is to this day. The answer to chaos, disorder, barrenness, and darkness is the declared Word of God. The seeds of change are in the Word itself.

THE DIVINE PRINCIPLE

*And God said, Let the earth bring forth grass, **the herb yielding seed**, and the fruit tree yielding fruit after his kind, **whose seed is in itself,** upon the earth: and it was so. And the earth brought forth grass, and herb yielding seed after his kind, and the tree yielding fruit, whose seed was in itself, after his kind: and God saw that it was good* (Genesis 1:11-12).

And God said, Let the earth bring forth the living creature after his kind, cattle, and creeping thing, and beast of the earth after his kind: and it was so. And God made the beast of the earth after his kind, and cattle after their kind, and every thing that creepeth upon the earth after his kind: and God saw that it was good (Genesis 1:24-25).

Notice in the first two verses the four references to seeds that replenish the earth. Also notice the eight times in these two passages that God says living things produce *after their kind.* "Kind" is the Hebrew word *miyn* and it means "species" (Strong, H4327). He is saying that living things produce their own species. They bring forth whatever they are.

The divine principle from the very beginning is, "Everything produces after its kind." God says *the seed is in itself,* meaning the kind of seed determines the kind of fruit that it produces. Without a seed there is no fruit, there are no animals, and no more humans can be born. Fruit comes from seeds, and every fruit produces after its kind. Apples always yield apples. Oranges always produce oranges. They don't get confused and produce something they are not. Apple seeds never produce peaches. The DNA in the seed determines what it is going to be—fruit, vegetation, the animal kingdom, trees, or man himself. By extension, you cannot plant evil and get good results. You cannot sow to the flesh and receive spiritual benefits. This divine principle applies to the spiritual world as much as the physical world. It's a law of creation, and it's never going to change.

SOWING AND REAPING

Paul wrote in Galatians 6:7-8 (NKJV), *"Do not be deceived, God is not mocked; for whatever a man sows, that he will also reap. For he who sows to his flesh will of the flesh reap corruption, but he who sows to the Spirit will of the Spirit reap everlasting life."* This reinforces the spiritual side of the principle—whatever is sown produces after its kind. "Whatever" is the Greek word *hos* meaning "this, that, other, or anything" (Strong, G3739). If you sow rebellion, you will reap rebellion. If you sow deceit, you are going to reap deceit. If you sow malice, you're going to receive malice. If you sow hatred, you will reap hatred in your life somehow. If you sow division, then disunity is going to start cropping up for you. If you sow an injustice, you will reap injustice at some point in your life. Conversely, if you sow love, then you will reap love. If you sow justice, you will be repaid with justice. If you sow kindness, you will receive kindness. Mercy, comfort, or helpfulness—those will be the fruit you reap in your life.

Carol and I have always tithed and we have always sown whatever we had, whatever we could. When we were building our first church and taking pledges to raise funds, we didn't really have any money to sow, so we gave what we had, which happened to be our wedding rings. We have always believed God's Word when it comes to giving, and He has never failed us. Many, many times we have given our entire paycheck to someone who needed it, knowing God would take care of our needs as well. We have even sown a car! We had a car we called "George," and there was a family in our church who needed a car to get to work. So we gave them George, and I walked to the church for work until God provided another car for us.

We have always given above and beyond the tithe; it's just a way of life for us—sowing and reaping. When we were students in Bible school, I was making $60 a week working at the salvage center in Dallas, and Carol made a few dollars babysitting children in our student apartment complex. There were many times when we had no idea how we were going to get our groceries, pay for our college books and tuition, and take care of our daughter, Rachel, who was three years old at the time. But we tithed anyway. We gave anyway, and God always provided. There would be a check in the mail from someone back home. We would open our Bible and there would be a $20 bill tucked inside. Someone would share a meal with us. Provision always came and still does. Sometimes it's not immediate, but sow anyway and in due season you will reap.

Sowing and reaping is not just financial. That's what we used this principle for, but we lost a great revelation because we kept it financial. Yes, financial seeds grow when planted in the Kingdom of God. Yes, money planted into God's church grows thirty-, sixty-, or one hundredfold. But *whatever* is sown is reaped. The focus of our life, as we live it out or plant it, will be reaped. We will harvest whatever we sow.

The early church understood this Scripture in ways that we do not. It's one we need to have a better understanding of today. It's a vital truth for success in the natural realm and the spirit realm. This revelation begins to show us God's original intent and purpose for man from the very beginning. It shows us the restored purpose of a born-again one, taking us back to the original design that Jesus restored to us on the cross.

BORN AGAIN

Seeing ye have purified your souls in obeying the truth through the Spirit unto unfeigned love of the brethren, see that ye love one another with a pure heart fervently: being born again, not of corruptible seed, but of incorruptible, by the word of God, which liveth and abideth for ever (1 Peter 1:22-23).

For you have been born again [that is, reborn from above— spiritually transformed, renewed, and set apart for His purpose] not of seed which is perishable but [from that which is] imperishable and immortal, that is, through the living and everlasting word of God (1 Peter 1:23 AMP).

Now that you've cleaned up your lives by following the truth, love one another as if your lives depended on it. Your new life is not like your old life. Your old birth came from mortal sperm; your new birth comes from God's living Word (1 Peter 1:22-23 MSG).

Moffatt's translation reads, *"You were born anew of immortal, not of mortal seed."* Kenneth Wuest's expanded translation says, *"Having been begotten again not of perishable seed but of imperishable, through the Word of God."*

A life conceived by God Himself opens up an area of potential and purpose that is so vast, it is mind boggling. The apostle Peter also describes God's Word as His seed. He takes us back to the very beginning to show us one of the most spectacular revelations man is ever going to receive. This incredible truth reveals God's fathering heart, yet few ever ponder it. Peter says the moment you received Jesus Christ as your Lord and Savior, God sowed His Spirit and His Word into your heart like a seed. You were born again by the incorruptible seed of the Word of God—not through corruptible seed but by the Holy Spirit and God's incorruptible Word sown into you or planted into you.

INCORRUPTIBLE SEED

This takes Christianity and being born again to levels few have dared to ponder, let alone live out. The believer in Jesus is made a new creature, a new species of being as the apostles clearly teach. This is not just some "feel good" statement. It is truth that changes everything. It separates Christianity from all other religions.

When our minds are renewed to this truth and we understand who we really are, it activates a royal priesthood mentality. A ruling species mentality. Few people even talk about this because it seems so grandiose, but we absolutely need a priesthood mentality in order to see great moves upon the earth. When we understand our place as a royal priesthood:

- Revival is going to surge through the nation.
- Whole nations can be discipled.
- We will demonstrate authority to rule and reign in this life, as Paul taught in Romans 5:17.
- We can activate and energize the dominion mandate of Genesis 1:26-28, commissioned by God Himself to go fulfill a certain purpose.
- The sons and daughters of God will act like sons and daughters of God.
- The authority of hell itself will not prevail against the people of God.

We will be fruitful. We will multiply. We will fill the earth, subdue it, and exercise our dominion in Christ's name within the parameters of His will.

CHILD OF GOD

You were born anew of incorruptible seed through the Word of God. The Greek word for "seed" is *spora,* and it's filled with new identity, new purpose, and new destiny (Strong, G4701). It also reveals the love of God for a son or a daughter, and it explains His combined affection and care for His new "born-gain" ones. It's a love that is real, pure, and constant. A love that caused the apostle John to exclaim in First John 3:1 (MSG), *"What marvelous love the Father has extended to us! Just look at it—we're called children of God! That's who we really are. But that's also why the world doesn't recognize us or take us seriously, because it has no idea who he is or what he's up to."*

Seed (*spora*) means parenting seed, fertilized seed, or activated seed containing genetic markers, codes, or traits. It means hereditary qualities and potentialities that are transmitted to offspring. A fertilized seed contains the parents' genetic markers. A parenting seed holds genetic codes and also generational markers.

The Holy Spirit conveys an incredible truth through the apostles about being born again. The moment you received Jesus as your Lord, God sowed His Spirit and His Word into your heart and you were born again by the incorruptible seed (*spora*) of God's Word. His parenting seed was sown into you and fertilized in your spirit. It was activated, germinated, and "lifed." Qualities and potentialities from God were transmitted to you, His offspring, much like how the seed in Mary's womb was fertilized, allowing Jesus to be supernaturally born of a virgin. You were born again—this time not through corruptible seed but by the Holy Spirit and God's incorruptible Word sown into you.

Now of course, God's seed sown into your heart produces God because it produces after its kind. It's a law of perpetuity. A God-seed produces His genetic codes in your spirit. You really are a son or daughter of God. New Testament teaching is clear, and it's affirming that the parenting seed of God is sown into you at the new birth. You have God-markers in you, literally! They are planted in the core of who you are. You are born of God.

GOD'S SEED

Through the parenting seed, character traits, mannerisms, tendencies, and likes or dislikes are passed on to the offspring. Preferences, actions, and hereditary dispositions are inherited through the parents' seed. This is true in our own family, as it is in yours. My daughter, Rachel, and I both can't talk without using our hands. We also have very similar temperaments. Our son, Joshua, is very much like his mother. They have similar personalities and leadership skills. Maddie, our oldest grandchild, for the most part acts like her dad, with a little bit of her mom thrown in. Our assistant, Katelyn, laughs and sounds like her mom when speaking. It's interesting and fun to notice these things.

If God's seed is in us, then certain tendencies of His will be passed on. It's why believers whose minds are renewed by God's Word can believe that miracles are still possible on the earth. Why? Because we're God's seed; we are His children, and He is the miracle-worker. It is sown into our new nature to have that leaning.

The world does not believe that all things are possible. But Christians whose minds are renewed by God's Word can easily believe such a thing. It's a hereditary trait inside of us. We tend to express power. Why? It's in our nature. It was seeded into us at our new birth. We tend to think with authority. We are predisposed that way because God's parenting seed is in us, and He is the highest authority. He has passed that on to us. We tend to believe for dominion, to see ourselves ruling, reigning, and conquering. These are hereditary leanings in the redeemed ones because we're God's seed. His disposition as the ruler of all is planted into us, into our nature, and it's very real. This is why First John 4:4 (AMP) says, *"You are of God and you belong to Him and have [already] overcome them [the agents of the antichrist]; because He who is in you is greater than he (satan) who is in the world [of sinful mankind]."* God is in us. He has planted His seed into us through His Word. His disposition to always overcome evil is planted into our very nature as a part of our spiritual DNA. He has seeded into the nature of His children to never give up but rather to subdue, conquer, and reign in Jesus' name.

There have been many situations in my life over the years when it would have been so much easier to just give up and quit. These times were so chaotic that others suggested that I give up and move on. But quitting is not in my born-again nature. It's not in the hereditary leanings my Father put into me. There is always the possibility to conquer and overcome with Him if I don't give up. Because of the hereditary nature deep inside of me, I didn't give up, and many times I won what was impossible in the natural realm. God put no losing seed in you!

When we made the shift from a local church to an apostolic hub, • there were quite a few who chose not to shift with us. They either didn't have a full understanding of where we were headed or they preferred a regular church. As a result, we lost a lot of people. During a time frame of several years, we had staff pastors leave as well as many people who had been with us from the beginning. It was a stressful time to say the least. Things looked impossible, especially in the financial realm. We had many friends and leaders advise us to just quit. There was so much debt, and many who had pledged to build with us had now abandoned us. We were still trying to figure out this apostolic call ourselves, let alone try to explain it to others. But we knew what God had said. One verse in particular sustained us through these times, and I would go to the church and stand and decree and declare it over and over again. *"I had fainted, unless I had believed to see • the goodness of the Lord in the land of the living"* (Ps. 27:13). In the face of what seemed to be insurmountable problems, we planted His Word in the heavens. God sustained us through this dark season, proving Himself faithful and true time and time again.

The tendency of God's kids is to think thoughts filled with hope. It's in the seed passed on to us. We don't need an outside source because we have an inner source. It's a well that springs up inside of us. Hope is a genetic marker inside of the redeemed, a genetic code in us if we will let it spring up. We are the offspring of the God of hope. That's true for every fruit of the Spirit. The fruit of the Spirit is the nature of God—love, joy, peace, longsuffering, gentleness, goodness, faith, meekness, and temperance (see Gal. 5:22-23). We don't need an outside source of joy. Joy is seeded inside of us. It's our tendency when we redeem our minds to be joyful no matter what is thrown our way. Peace is also seeded into us, living inside of us. When our mind is renewed, we have peace in the midst of our storms.

RACHEL'S STORY

In 2008, I found out I was pregnant, but didn't tell anyone—well, except for my husband. Usually, one finding out they're pregnant is exciting, joyful, and happy news. While I was all of those things, I was also filled with anxiousness, worry, and hesitation. This was my sixth pregnancy in five years. I had lost five precious babies. I was hopeful yet hesitant. That same week I found out, we were holding a large conference at our church and I was leading worship for each session. I knew it would be hard to be around so many people and not say anything, so I did end up telling my parents and one close friend.

They were very encouraging and supportive, knowing all I had been through. And honestly, it was a relief for them to know! I led each session and was filled with hope and peace spending time in the presence of our King. There was a time of prayer during one of the sessions, and I was told someone wanted to pray for me. The person praying for me said, "You have life in you. You will dance the dance of life."

She had *no idea* I was pregnant. But I knew the Holy Spirit was speaking through her in that moment. I clung to those words throughout my pregnancy. I decreed God's Word over my baby every day. "You will live and not die. My vine will not cast its fruit before its time. You give life and You give life abundantly. I stand on Your goodness and faithfulness."

And I did "dance the dance of life." I gave birth to a healthy baby boy after all those losses and all those years of mourning. God turned my mourning into joy. What was meant to keep me depressed, hopeless, and bitter, He turned to sweet and made me joyful and filled with hope. He taught my feet to dance for life, strength, and joy. My victory rests upon the promise of His Word. His plans for us are good, and He always gives us a future filled with hope. —Rachel Sheets Shafer

THE DANCE

Imagine you and the Lord Jesus are walking along the beach together. For much of the way, the Lord's footprints go along steadily, consistently, rarely varying the pace. But your footprints are a disorganized stream of zigzags, starts, stops, turnarounds, circles, departures, and returns. For much of the way, it seems to go like this, but gradually your footprints come more in line with the

Lord's, soon paralleling His consistently. You and Jesus are walking as true friends!

This seems perfect, but then an interesting thing happens. Your footprints that once etched the sand next to Jesus' are now walking precisely in His steps. Inside His large footprints are your small ones; you and Jesus are becoming one.

This goes on for many miles, but gradually you notice another change. The footprints inside the large footprints seem to grow larger. Eventually they disappear altogether. There is only one set of footprints; they have become one. This goes on for a long time, but suddenly the second set of footprints is back.

Zigzags all over the place. Stops, starts, gashes in the sand. A veritable mess of prints. This time it seems even worse! You are amazed and shocked. Your dream ends.

You pray, "Lord, I understand the first scene with the zigzags and fits. I was a new Christian, and I was just learning. But You walked on through the storm and helped me learn to walk with You."

And He spoke softly, "That is correct."

"And when the smaller footprints were inside of Yours, I was actually learning to walk in Your steps; I followed You very closely."

And He answered, "Very good. You have understood everything so far."

"When the smaller footprints grew and filled in Yours, I suppose that I was becoming like You in every way."

He beamed, "Precisely."

"So Lord, was there a regression or something? The footprints separated, and this time it was worse than before. Zigzags, gashes in the sand, turns every which way, circles."

There is a pause as the Lord answers with a smile in His voice, "You didn't know? That was when we danced!" — Author Unknown[1]

JOINT HEIRS WITH CHRIST

Have you ever wondered why you feel so different from the rest of the world? Do you ever think that those around you who are not born again seem like foreigners? It's like they speak a foreign language. Where did they come up with those crazy ideas? But you know they believe the things they say. Do you ever wonder why you think so differently? It's because you have inherited genetic leanings that cause you to think differently. You're God's seed, His child. It is in you to be different. In fact, if you live contrary to God's seed, your conscience is going to bother you because the Holy Spirit in you is going to say, "No, stop it. Don't do that. That's not who you are." You are His child.

Your Father's likes and dislikes have been passed on to you. God's character traits are at work in you, desiring to grow and mature. *You're an heir of God and a joint heir with Christ Jesus* (see Rom. 8:17). Renew your mind to it. Transform your thinking by meditating on who God's Word says you really are. Practice Paul's admonition in Romans 12:2 (AMP), *"And do not be conformed to this world [any longer with its superficial values and customs], but be transformed and progressively changed [as you mature spiritually] by the renewing of your mind [focusing on godly values and ethical attitudes], so that you may prove [for yourselves] what the will of God is, that which is good and acceptable and perfect [in His plan and purpose for you]."*

THE GOD DYNASTY

We need to reprogram our minds to think like children of God. To think like one born into a dynasty family of governing authority—the God dynasty. We must think like one living the mandate of God to exercise dominion upon the earth in His name, activating real Christian living. Amazingly, God wants to reproduce Himself in you. He wants His image, likeness, and life to grow in you. He wants you to rule and reign with Him. You were born of God to have dominion, not to be dominated by hell, society, culture, or government. Your DNA reads *Overcomer.* Your DNA says *Dominator.* Your DNA declares *Ruler with my Father.* He wants you to be an activated heir, restored in purpose and identity as His offspring to create with words that agree with His words. Like your Father, you as a child of God create with words that are seeds.

As His seed on the earth, He wants you to create with "word seed" decrees—create atmospheres for miracles, parameters for society to live in, and an environment that produces life and destroys death. Father God wants His seed in you to release His creative abilities upon the earth. That's why demons try to keep you silent! That's why hell wants to shut you up.

CREATIVE DNA

Philippians 2:13 shouts this grace-filled truth: *"For it is God which worketh in you to will and to do of his good pleasure."* J.B. Rotherham's translation says, *"For it is, God, who energiseth within you, both the desiring and the energising, in behalf of his good pleasure."* God's seed in you energizes you to create God's will by decreeing His Word. His seed becomes a creative force in the heavens and the earth when decreed by those who have His DNA, His *spora.* It is His plan that when His heirs open their mouth, creative spheres will open. Power to change things and bring order out of chaos will be released. Your spirit has been seeded with the DNA and nature of the living God.

God wants to energize His creative nature in you. You have been redeemed and restored to create with word seeds. Your words can create openings for God's purpose upon the earth and His will in the nations. Your words plant the heavens with divine principles and create an environment for them to exist on the earth. The dominion mandate is not some phantom mandate that God has forgotten about. It is an eternal principle. It is expected that God's redeemed ones will rule, reign, and exercise dominion in Jesus' name. It is Godhead-approved. It has His Kingdom and angel armies backing it. (We will learn more about the dominion mandate in Chapter 3.)

The mandate includes the restoring of our words as seeds aligned with God's. Our words:

- produce after their kind,
- produce what those words say,
- subdue God's enemies,
- produce God's promises,
- restore our voices as God's heirs.

We can seed the heavens with the Words of God, creating change and releasing His power. We can extend His rule on the earth by planting the heavens with energized, activated words.

Those who are born-again ones, who have had God's seed sown into them, can now declare words that are seeds just like He did. It's a part of who we are. It's a part of the newborn nature God passed on. Our words spoken in faith in Christ's name become seeds that produce after their kind. Our words in His name are anointed to come to pass. We are to rule with them.

WORD SEED DECREES

In the beginning, God said *"be"* and it was. *"Trees be,"* and they were. The words produced after their kind. *"Sun be,"* and the sun was. That word produced after its kind. He planted the heavens and the earth with word seed decrees. Now, we have been restored because of Calvary, because of the cross, to plant word seed decrees. We are to make decrees of faith based on God's Word and His will. We have been reborn to say "be" to things. "Be" to things that need to be done, "be" to things that need to be produced. It is time for us to be who we really are. The world is crying out for the manifestation of the sons and daughters of God. It's time to recognize that we have God's traits passed on to us. We are heirs with authority delegated to us to be a ruling species of beings. Father's DNA is in us.

My earthly father and mother passed on genetics that can still be seen in me today. But my spirit has God's DNA in it. I am God's son—I really am! *Son* is not just some word that sounds really nice. I am here as His offspring to decree His words of life, power, and change— words that produce after their kind. Words that plant the heavens and the earth with God's Word. Word seeds that become what God says. I am here to follow the ways of my Father who has passed them on to me. It is in my spirit. It has been fertilized, germinated, and activated inside of me.

It's time we use our God-given rights as heirs of Christ to decree words that seed change everywhere. Word seed decrees that disciple a nation. Word seed decrees that declare God's power, scatter darkness, and bring order out of chaos just like His Word did in the beginning. Just like Dad did. Holy Spirit hovers until He hears God's seed declared, God's Word voiced. He's hovering today over a nation and the world, waiting for the sons and daughters of God to become the voice of God on this planet and declare His Word and not back down. It's in us to do it.

If you have confessed Jesus as Lord, He has germinated His nature as a seed inside of you. You really are a child of God. A part of your restored purpose is to seed the world with His words. Never speak negative words or unbelief. They are contrary to the seed of God that is in you. Reign in His name, speaking words of life and revival. We are here as His sons and His daughters to voice His Word everywhere. The greatest days in church history are not in our past; they are in our present and in our future. Say what God says.

NOTE

1. Quoted in Dutch Sheets, *The Power of Hope* (Lake Mary, FL: Charisma House, 2014), 80–82.

CHAPTER

2

PLANTING THE HEAVENS

And I have put My words in your mouth; I have
covered you with the shadow of My hand, that I
may plant the heavens, lay the foundations of the
earth, and say to Zion, "You are My people."
—ISAIAH 51:16 NKJV

Isaiah 51:16 speaks revelation to us right now, in this day and time. However, the fullness of what God was saying to the prophet Isaiah is not going to be manifested until He comes back in His millennial reign. Notice He says, *"I have put My words in your mouth."* The word for "mouth" is the Hebrew word *peh*, and it means the taste center of the body (Strong, H6310). You eat food by putting it in your mouth, chewing it up, and swallowing it. Where words are concerned, the mouth is literally the speech center of the body.

Peh also has a figurative meaning—the opening of the body to sound forth a command, an instruction, a prophetic word or insight, or some other communication. The mouth does this by forming and amplifying words to a person, organization, congregation, nation, government, or other similar entity. God distinguishes two different realms where the words take effect, realms not talked about very much in our times but clearly emphasized by God right from the beginning—the heavens or the earth.

PRAYERS ARE WORD SEEDS

In this verse in Isaiah, God talks about words sounding forth from the mouths of His sons and daughters, His heirs, into the realm of the heavens or the earth. This again emphasizes that words are seeds—word seed decrees. This also includes prayer because prayers are words of communication seeded into the heavens and into the earth. Prayer is speech to God making a request, but it is also, at times, a decree of God's promises. Prayers express confidence in God's answering abilities, or they may ask for divine intervention into a situation.

The mouth (*peh*) is the opening of the body to sound forth God's Word as seeds that grow to fullness until they are manifested in the heavens or in the earth. The mouth is, therefore, the opening through which we sow the seed of God's Word into a region. Lucifer and his kingdom seek to silence Christ's body (the Church). They want our mouths closed. They don't want us to speak. Part of a demon's assignment is to shut the mouth of Christ's body. Too many in the Body of Christ have fallen into that error and actually embraced it.

From the very beginning, God's original intent was for His sons and daughters, His heirs, to open their mouths and declare His words into the earth. He has put His Word in your mouth so that He may plant it in the heavens and the earth. The word for "plant" is the Hebrew word *nata*, and it means to plant, to fix, or to set in place (Strong, H5193). God Himself was the original Gardener, and we have inherited that job from Him as His heirs.

GRANDPA'S GARDEN

Whenever I think about planting, I think of my grandfather Henkel. He worked at a hardware store in Waverly, Ohio, and he needed to make extra income. For probably 25 years or so, he would sell plants in the spring. He always began the process in the winter time. I can remember, as a little kid, my grandpa sitting in the living room flipping through books of seeds and wondering aloud, "Do I want this kind of tomato plant?" "Is this the kind of seed I'm going to buy?" He would decide what kinds of seeds he was going to order. Then, as soon as the weather broke, he would go out into what he called "hot beds," which were four or five feet wide and ten feet long, and that's where he planted everything. He would dig up all the dirt and he would burn it and mix in fertilizer and then he would go out and plant those seeds. He would cover the seeds up with plastic, and he was careful to water them and take care of them. When those plants got to maybe six to eight inches tall, he would put up his sign on the front porch: "Plants for Sale."

People came from all around Waverly, Ohio, to buy my grandpa's plants. My grandfather's seeds planted a lot of gardens in Waverly. Hundreds of people ate from them. People would come and get the little plants that he would wrap in newspaper, and they would take them home to their gardens and set them out. Of course, he saved some of the plants to set out in his own garden. He always had one of the best gardens anywhere around, and he fed his family out of that garden year round. Whatever they didn't eat they would can and save for later.

GOD'S SPOKEN WORDS

In the beginning, God planted the stars. His Word said *"be"* and it was. He set the stars, sun, and planets into place. He planted galaxies and moons with His Word. He planted the heavens and he planted the earth with His word seed decrees. He told the prophet Isaiah in Isaiah 51:16, "I have put My words in your mouth that I might plant the heavens and lay the foundations of the earth." Foundations on the earth were established according to God's decreed word. The condition of the heavens and the earth were dependent upon the Word of God, His spoken word, and it still is today.

The entire universe is made to hearken to the voice of God's Word. Heaven and earth are made to respond to the voice of God's Word. Angel armies are made to respond to the voice of God's Word. Amazingly, human beings, made in God's image and likeness, are also carriers of God's voice when they are activated at the new birth. As His seed on the earth, we are to open our mouths and plant the heavens and the earth with God's Word. We are to declare the words of God into the heavens and the earth, mankind, nations, government, congregations, and people everywhere to set in place foundations for stable government and society. We are to be stewards of what God said was to be. If the foundations are not set according to God's Word, then at some point that society is going to crumble under the weight of iniquitous roots. Jesus said that such a house will not be built upon rock; it will be built upon sand, and when the storm comes it is going to fall (see Matt. 7:26).

The Body of Christ is to open their mouths and plant God's Word into the earth. Like my grandfather planted produce (good seeds) into all of Waverly, we, too, are to plant God's good word seeds into our cities and regions. "I have put My words in your mouth that I might plant the heavens and the earth." Words are the seeds we plant with.

PLANTING WORDS IN A REGION

Years ago, before I ever understood that words are seeds, I remember I was asked to go to a very small church in southern Ohio. I knew the pastor, and they had a special event going on and wanted me to come share. I don't remember what the event was, but I remember praying, "OK, Lord. What should I share with these people?" As I prayed about, it I received revelation concerning the church ruling and reigning with Christ Jesus in this life (see Rom. 5:17). I got a download of understanding and it just kept coming. Afterward I began to think, "I need to help the Lord out here." It's something I don't attempt to do much anymore, but I said, "Lord, that's not what these people need to hear. They won't understand this. This is not even on their radar screen. This is not where they're at."

He said something to me all those years ago that I have never forgotten, and it has been instruction for me concerning my apostolic calling and assignment ever since. He said, *"They will understand what I help them to understand and what I reveal to their hearts."* In other words, don't you worry about them getting fed—I will take care of that.

I have seen that over the years. I don't know how many times I have preached a sermon and somebody has come up and said, "That is exactly what I needed to hear," and proceeded to tell me what they got from the message. In the meantime, I'm thinking, "That is not even what I said! It's not even my point!" But it was God's point to them. However many people are there, that's how many sermons you're preaching because they're thinking concerning their own life situations, their own experiences, and what God is saying to them.

God said, "They'll understand what I help them understand and what I reveal to their hearts." But then He said, *"I need you to plant this word into the region."*

Now that gave me pause. I began to think, "Can I do that? Lord, can I plant a message in the heavens and the earth realm of a region? Do You really want me to plant a message, to plant doctrine from Your Word into the atmosphere of a region?"

Very clearly He said to me, "Yes. I want to grow it there. It has been requested by My people, and I need you to sow it into the region. I need you to set the foundations. I need you to lay the biblical foundation for it. It's what apostles and prophets do." I remember thinking at the time, "They do? I didn't know that." Then the Scripture came to mind that the church is built upon the foundation of the apostles and the prophets (see Eph. 2:20). He clearly said, *"I need you to sow this into the region."*

SEEDING THE ATMOSPHERE

I had never thought about it. It had never crossed my mind. I had never heard anybody else talk about this. But I knew a new level of understanding was being given to me, one that years later would help me with my apostolic calling. Sometimes when I am preaching, I will have the awareness that while I am talking God is going to help people understand or get something out of it, but I am also seeding the atmosphere of a region. I'm preaching a message, but I am really planting revival seeds everywhere. I'm planting God's will into the region. I am setting the foundations in the spirit realm. Sometimes I feel like I am laying a foundation in the spirit realm or into the atmosphere so that there can be productivity. I am preaching and planting the heavens. I'm preaching and planting the earth, in and around this country, for reformation and awakening.

So many times I have the awareness that God is saying, "Plant this into the region. Don't worry about it. Just plant it into the spirit realm. I want to grow it there. It's been requested by My people." Some Sunday mornings, on my way to speak, I experience understanding and begin to think, *"I'm preaching this one to seed the region. I am preaching this to seed into the state. I am preaching this to seed it into the atmosphere of the United States of America."* It's not always that way, but sometimes it is. I had to learn that. It is something apostles and prophets do, but it is also something all sons and daughters are supposed to do—apostles and prophets just model it.

BUILDING A FIREWALL

This has helped me with the AwakeningNow Prayer Network, which we began in Ohio in 2008 and is spreading into the surrounding states. This network now has hundreds of churches in the region. The word from Prophet Chuck Pierce was, "Build a firewall around the entire state."

I didn't know how to build a firewall around the whole state, but in prayer the Holy Spirit said, "Go to all eighty-eight counties and hold prayer assemblies." We are currently doing that—we take apostolic teams and worship teams to the prayer assemblies and we make 50 or 60 decrees into that county.

We are there to plant God's Word in the heavens and the earth of that region, and we do that with bold, faith-filled decrees of what God says. We plant prophetic words into that region. We plant that region with the will of God. We, along with the remnant believers who gather, are there to sow the atmosphere of that region with God's word seed decrees so that the rains of Heaven can come and activate them and grow them to fullness. In a sense, we are planting gardens everywhere—gardens that will be beautiful and feed and bless the people of God. Without this understanding of words as seeds or praying into the atmosphere, there is little doubt that I would be doing what I am now doing.

PLANTING THE HEAVENS

This method of planting the heavens was also taught by Jesus. Remember that He first planted the heavens and the earth in Genesis 1. He is the Word. He planted the entire universe with word seed decrees, saying "be" and it was. In Matthew 6:10 (NKJV), He taught us to pray this way, *"Your kingdom come. Your will be done on earth as it is in heaven."* That's a different kind of prayer because it's not really a petition—it's a declaration. It's not a foretelling of the future—it's a commanding decree. It's calling something to be, calling something to exist. In other words, He said to declare, "Will of God, be done. Will of God, come."

When Jesus walked the earth, we see that His words just caused things to happen. Wherever He went, He opened His mouth and He sounded forth decrees that brought miraculous results. In John 6:63 (NKJV) He tells us, saying this, *"The words that I speak to you are spirit, and they are life."* Understand the magnitude of that statement. When Christ spoke, when He opened His mouth and decreed, Holy Spirit moved into the atmosphere. His mouth opened the atmosphere for Holy Spirit to begin to move. Remember, Holy Spirit hovers until He hears the Word of God. When He hears the Word of God declared, He moves, just like He did upon the chaos and darkness in the beginning. Christ's mouth opened ways for the Kingdom to come. His mouth proclaimed an invitation, "Holy Spirit come. Move here."

What Jesus said produced after its kind. The superior reality of the Kingdom of God, a spiritual Kingdom that visibly affects the entire earth, began to move and transform the earth realm. The Word became a reality and produced what He decreed. The seed in the words produced it. Jesus was modeling ministry for you and me, His joint heirs.

JOINT HEIRS

For you did not receive the spirit of bondage again to fear, but you received the Spirit of adoption by whom we cry out, "Abba, Father." The Spirit Himself bears witness with our spirit that we are children of God, and if children, then

heirs—heirs of God and joint heirs with Christ, if indeed
we suffer with Him, that we may also be glorified together
(Romans 8:15-17 NKJV).

"Joint heirs" is the Greek word *sygkleronomos,* and it simply means a coheir (Strong, G4789). It is also the Greek word for "identical." We are *identical heirs* with Christ. Because of God's grace and the free gift of righteousness through the cross, believers (born-again ones) have now been made to be identical heirs with Christ Jesus. Christ mentors those heirs (us) through the example of His earthly life, showing us how to open our mouths and sound forth spirit-alive words. Yes, we as coheirs can speak with the presence of the power of the Holy Spirit and can plant the heavens and the earth realms. That's staggering. That's hard to get your mind around.

When the sons and daughters of God open their mouths and decree God's Word, it can change the atmosphere of a region. Our decrees act as a catalyst that sets in motion a chain of events to bring God's Word to pass. They open the heavens so blessings can rain down, miracles can be produced, and we can receive revelation and enlightenment. Our decrees attract angel armies to ascend and descend and assist the heirs of salvation in that region (see Heb. 1:14).

As God's heirs, as His children on the earth, we are commissioned to plant the heavens with His words, to seed them with declarations of truth. We must declare, on the basis of God's Word, the rightful rule of King Jesus over the earth, the region, and over the kingdom of darkness. We are commissioned to do it. It is well past time, but the sons and daughters of God are just waiting for Christ's return, just waiting for Him to come back. We are commanded to occupy until He comes (see Luke 19:13). We are commanded to rule and reign with Him in this life (see Rom. 5:17). We are to rule over principalities and powers, mights and dominions of darkness, binding them with superior authority just like Jesus bound them when He opened His mouth and declared that they must go. Sitting silent with closed mouths has never been an option for real heirs.

CREATE WITH WORDS

In Isaiah 55, God tells us that His declared word becomes creative. This now starts to get very interesting. Just as God created with His words, saying *"be"* and it was, so you and I, His legitimate seeds on the earth, are restored in purpose and identity to create with our words. Our words, in alignment with God's Word when declared in faith, become creative seeds that grow and produce after their kind. Our words become creative when they are in agreement with God's Word and in alignment with Holy Spirit and His revelation to us. They open creative spheres in a region. Think about it—how could God's creative seed literally be placed in you and you not be creative in nature? The Creator seed is in us; it is our nature to be creative with our words.

> For as the heavens are higher than the earth, so are My ways higher than your ways, and My thoughts than your thoughts. For as the rain comes down, and the snow from heaven, and do not return there, but water the earth, and make it bring forth and bud, that it may give seed to the sower and bread to the eater, so shall My word be that goes forth from My mouth; it shall not return to Me void, but it shall accomplish what I please, and it shall prosper in the thing for which I sent it (Isaiah 55:9-11 NKJV).

> It is the same with my word. I send it out, and it always produces fruit. It will accomplish all I want it to, and it will prosper everywhere I send it (Isaiah 55:11 NLT).

So will My word be which goes out of My mouth; it will not return to Me void (useless, without result), *without accomplishing what I desire, and without succeeding in the matter for which I sent it* (Isaiah 55:11 AMP).

So will the words that come out of my mouth not come back empty-handed. They'll do the work I sent them to do, they'll complete the assignment I gave them (Isaiah 55:11 MSG).

GOD'S PROMISE TO US

Words are given assignments! What a promise! "My words shall not return void." "Return" is the Hebrew word *shuv,* and it means "turn around" (Strong, H7725). The promise to you and me—the born-again ones, His sons and daughters—is that the word you decree will not turn around. It cannot be reversed. It's not going to boomerang. The word for "not" is the Hebrew word *lo,* and it simply means to negate something (Strong, H3808). It's a particle of negation in the Hebrew language. It makes a positive statement negative. For example, *"I am absolutely going to do this, maybe."* That's *lo.*

Hear this: God says, "There are not going to be any maybes or I won'ts. If I said it, that's what's going to happen. If it's My word decreed, it's not going to be turned around on you. It shall not be negated. Hell will not negate it. Lucifer will not negate it. Government won't negate it. Demons won't negate it. Humanism cannot negate it. Nothing can negate it."

The word for "void" is the Hebrew word *raykawm,* and it means empty, ineffectual, and to leak out (Strong, H7387). God says, "My word that My sons and daughters decree in My name does not return empty." In other words, He is saying, "I don't give empty promises. No, they're all full. They're all effective, and they do not leak. They don't leak out." He tells Isaiah and He tells us today, *"My promises don't leak. They never return empty."*

"It shall accomplish" is one word in the Hebrew text and it's the word *asah*, meaning to yield out of oneself (Strong, H6213). That's what God does—He brings out of Himself. He creates from within Himself with His words. That's what Hebrews 11:3 is talking about. *"Through faith we understand that the worlds were framed by the word of God, so that things which are seen were not made of things which do appear."*

The entire universe came out of God. All of creation came out of God. His words framed it. His words decreed it and described it and it produced its kind. All visible, material things were decreed by God to be. They all came out of Him as He decreed His words as seeds. Of course, if the whole universe came out of God then most certainly He can create whatever we need. How hard can that be? Our God can create any word that He speaks. No word of His is empty. When we decree God's Word, creative forces begin to flow. Even if what is needed doesn't exist, God's Word can create it.

The word *asah* also means to become, to come to pass, to yield, or to bear (Strong, H6213). *Asah* draws a picture of a fruit tree—it will yield whatever kind it is. The seed contains the tree that will grow from it. The fruit is also in the seed and it becomes what it is. *Asah* is also the word for "execute" or "furnish." God's Word is furnished with power to execute and to bring that word to pass. God's Word, when decreed by His seed in alignment with His will, becomes what it is. God says it will prosper in the thing for which He sent it. "Prosper" is the Hebrew word *tsaleach*, and it means to push forward, to break out, to be good, to be successful, or to be profitable (Strong, H6743). God's Word decreed becomes profitable. It breaks out of confinement. That's the way soil is pictured in the Scriptures. Soil is a confinement for the seed, but the seed breaks out of confinement to produce what it is. Word seeds break through blockages in the heavens and the earth and they are made good. They are successful. They yield and release creative abilities.

THE POWER OF OUR DECREES

We have to understand the power in our decrees of God's Word. We almost haven't even dared to go there. Perhaps it seems too good to be true because we are accustomed to living with a negative theology that we are just downtrodden Christians waiting for Jesus to come. If that's how we think, we have not understood who we really are and who God made us to be. We have not realized that His DNA is literally transmitted into us. Our decrees, just like Jesus Christ's decrees (our identical heir), can become creative forces that break openings in the heavens or the earth for God's purpose and His plan to produce.

We have this promise: when we stand in faith and decree what God says; when we refuse to back off; when we refuse to abandon that word seed; when we water the seed with our faith, our prayers, our praise, our confession, and our steadfast trust, the seed will produce after its kind. It becomes what it is or what it describes. Never give up on a seed you plant. Never give up on God's Word. Never. Don't negate it. We are supposed to make decrees that break loose hell's grip. We can bring forth God's promises in fullness upon the earth.

As God's sons and daughters, we ought to walk this planet expecting to reap God's abundant life that His word describes to us. We should expect:

- God's word seeds that we decree to produce after their kind
- The word of promise to come to pass, no matter what it is

- The word seeds we sow to become fruitful and multiply

- God's Word on healing to produce the fruit of healing

- His Word that we decree on good success to bear the fruit of success

We should walk this planet declaring the promise and purpose of God and what His Word says. This is true in all aspects of our lives— for example, parenting. My wife, Carol, shared the following story with me that she found on Joanna Gaines' Facebook page. Joanna and Chip Gaines are the popular hosts of HGTV's *Fixer Upper* (a show I have never seen). Joanna writes:

> There's an Adonis Blue butterfly bush I planted by the girls' window almost five years ago when we were renovating the farmhouse. I wanted butterflies by the girls' windows that they could see and enjoy. I never told them about the bush and, honestly, I forgot about it over the years.
>
> This morning, I found my little Emmie sitting by her window, looking excitedly at the bush and saying, "Here she is! My little hummingbird comes every morning, Mom!" First, I didn't know she looked out for her bird every morning. Second, I forgot all about the bush and never told her if she looked out the window she would see the prettiest butterflies and hummingbirds gathered around it.
>
> It's hard not to think, this is a lot like parenting. You sow seeds early on and work hard to be intentional and then, over time, you move on to new lessons and challenges. Then one day you look up and the seeds you planted in your little children's hearts are now in full bloom. Be

encouraged today to keep pressing in and tending to their hearts. It will be worth it. —Joanna Gaines[1]

Parenting seeds planted are still growing years later; even as an adult they are still there.

We should expect deliverance, freedom, prosperity, harvest, miracles, healings, signs, wonders, favor, strength, restoration, satisfaction, fullness, preservation, ways provided for us, help provided for us, abundance to come our way, rest for our souls, and wisdom for answers. Why? It is the seed that is in you. It's the nature of God. Remember, God's *spora* is in you. Expect the parenting seed of your Father to produce His nature. Expect His Word to produce His life everywhere. Expect bountiful gardens to come up all around you to feed and prosper your life. Words are seeds. They grow and they become after their kind.

Prophet Chuck Pierce recently released this prophetic word, which illustrates the importance of your words as seeds:

> Many seeds have been planted, and many seeds are now waiting for a chance in the atmosphere so they can sprout. These seeds are not lying desolate but are waiting for an atmosphere of refreshing and rejoicing that will cause them to break forth. This is a time I'm sending out those who will go to those places where seeds are sown, and from the seeds being sown they will open a portal so the rain of My Spirit can come. Then they will harvest and bring back to the storehouse what needs to be brought back. Seeds are waiting. Your portal will carry the water to bring forth the harvest of grain that has fallen into the earth for a season of death. From the death of past fields a great harvest will come! Amen!

NOTE

1. Joanna Gains' Facebook page, accessed March 15, 2017, https://www.facebook.com/JoannaStevensGaines/?fref=nf.

CHAPTER

3

THE DOMINION
MANDATE

Then God said, "Let Us make man in Our image,
according to Our likeness; let them have dominion over
the fish of the sea, over the birds of the air, and over
the cattle, over all the earth and over every creeping
thing that creeps on the earth." So God created man
in His own image; in the image of God He created
him; male and female He created them. Then God
blessed them, and God said to them, "Be fruitful and
multiply; fill the earth and subdue it; have dominion
over the fish of the sea, over the birds of the air, and
over every living thing that moves on the earth."
—GENESIS 1:26-28 NKJV

As we continue to dive into these waters of revelation, we see that
God says His born-again ones who decree His Word as seed are given

dominion. *Dominion* is not a bad word. We just have to understand it in balance with the Scripture. The seeds, the sons and daughters of God, are given dominion and are meant to subdue the earth according to what God has said. Seeds dominate earth. Earth does not dominate seed. You can plant a seed into the earth—bury it in a dirt grave—but it will resurrect. It will dominate the soil. The seed has dominion over the earth. It will overcome what buries it and will break out. When believers plant God's Word into the heavens or into the earth, it will break through and produce. It will dominate what attempts to bury it and produce after its kind.

When God's sons and daughters plant His Word, the seed's dominion is activated and it will break out of all confinements and produce. It will prosper. Just give a seed a little bit of time, give it a few days, and the seed will begin to push through and reveal its dominion. It will sprout, bud, and grow to fullness. It will mature and prosper, and the earth will support it. The seed isn't there to support the earth; the earth nourishes the seed. It's designed to collaborate with the Word of God that we sow, and it will assist the seed to be what it is.

THE DOMINION MANDATE

Genesis 1:26-28 is commonly called *the dominion mandate*. God gave a divine purpose to man from the very beginning of creation. He commissioned man by saying, "You are here to be fruitful, multiply, and subdue the earth and have dominion over everything in it." It is highly significant that the first thing God said to Adam and Eve was, "I want you to rule the earth for Me. I am authorizing you to govern. Societies will need government. See to it. Plant My Word everywhere, and dominion will be activated."

Knowing who God is, we can conclude that He meant to say that. He didn't accidentally say that a part of your purpose is governing. He didn't say, "Oh wait, I'm not warmed up yet. We've started? Whoops, let's start over." No, He meant this. It was His will for His imaged ones to rule and reign on the earth. That was His original intent, and you must understand what this means if you are ever going to clearly understand purpose. Why? Because hell has done everything it can to distort God's purpose so that hell's kingdom, not God's Kingdom, can rule the earth.

When lucifer led a *coup d'état* trying to take over Heaven, the battle was over governance—who was going to rule? Would God rule or lucifer? The same is true today. Lucifer wants to subdue man and govern the earth. He disrupted God's plan by tempting man to sin, corrupting God's purpose *until* Christ came with His Kingdom to reconcile man back to God through His sacrifice on Calvary's cross.

ORIGINAL INTENT

Christ's death and resurrection reactivated God's original intent for His born-again ones. He restored lost purpose and purposes, and He reactivated the dominion mandate. We've got to understand that God has not changed His mind. His purpose still stands. No purpose of God can ultimately fail. It might be disrupted, but it is going to resurrect and the purpose of God will always be done.

Jesus came and redeemed us from the fall of man in Genesis. He restored us back to God and clothed us in His righteousness. Christian is the born-again one who is now in right standing with God. When Christ rose from the dead, having finished the sacrifice for man's redemption, He repeated the same words that the Godhead originally spoke to man in the beginning. In Matthew 28:18, He arose from the dead saying, *"All authority has been given to Me in heaven and on earth."* In other words, "Now you reign in My name. All authority has been given to me. I delegate it to you—now you rule. You reign. You govern. You have dominion." He commanded us, "You, disciple nations. Become My Kingdom government upon the earth."

Through the cross, reconciliation came to us. The born-again ones are to be ministers of reconciliation (see 2 Cor. 5:18). This includes, among many things, reforming nations and fighting to change the culture. It involves laws, societal standards, and government. It is God's purpose, plan, and intent that we do so. This purpose has not changed. Part of the mandate is to *subdue,* but most of today's church has quietly suppressed that idea. As a result, the original intent is not fully understood in our times. Instead, the exact opposite is taught in much of the Body of Christ today. Obviously, we are going to need to know the full truth if we are ever going to see it work for us.

THE FALL OF MAN

The apostle Paul describes the fall of man as a fall from truth in Romans 1. When Adam and Eve ate the forbidden fruit it was evident that they believed the enemy's lie. When you believe a lie you empower the liar—every time. That's why we must state the truth clearly—because we are being lied to. The media, universities, and governments are lying to us. They are attempting to rewrite our history, the history of our nations, with lies and deception. Agreeing with the devil empowers him, giving him license to kill, steal, and destroy. It gives him license to govern.

When Adam and Eve ate the forbidden fruit they denied the truth. They cut the ground out from under themselves, and they fell when they decided to abandon God's perspective for a distortion. The church has done the exact same thing. She has accepted a distortion of God's perspective on our purpose. It was true then and it is true today—suppressing the truth causes rampant foolishness. Suppressing the truth causes darkness of heart and allows demons to rule, handing authority over to the devil just as Adam and Eve did.

The tactic of lucifer and his kingdom has always been to suppress truth. It's how he usurps authority. It's not new. He has always done it that way. It's a strategy that you can easily see in our world today. The truth that America is a Christian nation is being suppressed, even though there are thousands of documents that say otherwise. In the 1800s, the Supreme Court ruled that we are a Christian nation, but that truth is suppressed. The truth that our nation is founded upon Scripture is being suppressed. There are those who are trying to purge it from our history books, and our colleges are teaching the exact opposite of that. Sadly, sound doctrine is also being suppressed in nominal churches everywhere.

Churches by the thousands have suppressed the truth through perverted doctrines of demons and through man's ideas. Humanism has now mingled with Christian doctrine and has perverted it. The homosexual agenda has replaced God's original intent for marriage. The doctrine of inclusion, which states that everybody is saved, has the potential to damn millions. Chrislam, a blend of Christianity and Islam, is now being embraced as politically correct. Tolerance for human ideas has distorted the perspective of God's purpose for man.

God's true sons and daughters must rise in their authority and declare God's Word as commanded. The true church must sow righteousness into the nation according to God's Word. We must also see a remnant arise and subdue, as originally intended. Unless a remnant declares the uncompromised truth of the Word of God, hell's kingdom will suppress truth, usurp authority, and rule our land through the unrighteous. We clearly see in Scriptures that this is the exact opposite of God's plan.

DISTORTED PERSPECTIVE OF REALITY

When Adam and Eve sinned, they fell from God's perspective of reality. Before they allowed satan to suppress the truth, they had unbroken access to God, His nature, His ways, and His intentions for them on the earth. Their purpose couldn't have been clearer. God described everything to them. But when they suppressed the truth of who God is, what He told them became twisted. Remember, that was lucifer's attack. He convinced them that God didn't really say those things and that God didn't want them to be like Him. Their own image of themselves, who they were, became warped, distorted, and deformed. This wrong perspective separated them from the two things they as humans needed in order to find fulfillment—their identity and purpose.

Sadly, millions of Christians still live in this distorted reality today. They are perishing for a lack of knowledge and truth. They are alive, but they have a distorted perspective and identity. At the fall of man, humanity's perspective inherited of God's nature and His intentions became misshapen. Adam and Eve's offspring inherited this distorted perspective of reality, giving them a perverted understanding of how the earth was to be ruled. That perpetuated the loss of identity and purpose. This reality became a continuing cycle for unsaved man. History reveals that when you do not have identity and purpose, confusion always reigns. Man does what is right in his or her own eyes. They are gods to themselves, and rampant lawlessness becomes the rule.

OUR IDENTITY

Thankfully, we now live in a time when the breach of sin has been healed by the cross. Thank God for the cross! Jesus came to redeem us from the fall and restore our broken relationship with God. Those who receive Jesus as Lord and Savior are born again and remade in Christ's likeness because of the cross. That's what *Christian* means— Christ-like ones. At the new birth we are refigured, reformed, restored, and reborn in our spirits. When we are made new, God activates our identity and purpose as He originally intended. We are restored and reconciled to Him. God's Word says that our redemption is the truth of our salvation.

The church has done a pretty good job of grasping the truth concerning our identities. We are heirs of God and joint heirs with Christ, sons and daughters of God, and the righteousness of Him in Christ Jesus. We have destiny and purpose, and Heaven is our ultimate home. Who we are in Christ has been taught for decades. But the truth is still suppressed that those who have been remade in His image are to rule the earth. It's dispensationalized as something that will occur far off in the future.

When the commandment came to Adam and Eve to fill the earth, to subdue it, and to have dominion, God was not referring to a millennial reign thousands of years later. He was referring to right then. It was a "now" word. It was original intent. We must understand that the moment God forgave us, He reactivated His original plan for us. We embrace this in almost every other area, but not in the authority and governing realm.

GOVERNING MANDATE

In the dominion mandate, God said, *"Be fruitful and multiply; fill the earth and subdue it"* (Gen. 1:28 NKJV). "Subdue" is the Hebrew word *kabash,* and it means to conquer, rule, and to bring into subjection (Strong, H3533). "Dominion" is the Hebrew word *radaah,* and it means to rule, to reign, to govern, and to take over (Strong, H7287). Of course, two people were not enough to govern the entire earth. They could rule their garden, but it would take millions of others to rule their own gardens if this was going to really be accomplished.

In Romans 5:17, the Apostle Paul said that we are to reign in life through Jesus Christ. Clearly, God wanted the earth filled with those made in His image who would bring the earth under the influence of

His Kingdom. He wanted a Kingdom. He wanted His sons and His daughters ruling with Him, walking in right relationship with Him and exercising their delegated authority on the earth. Earth, not some spiritual dimension only. Not something in the heavens only. It's vital that we understand what is being said here because we are losing the soul of a nation due to lack of understanding.

"Earth" is the Hebrew word *erets,* and it means land(s), country, fields, nation(s), the physical planet, territory (Strong, H776). Have we suppressed the truth that God wants us to rule territories, nations, countries, lands all across this earth? Yes, we have. It's become the perspective of most of our world now and most Christians also. We have allowed the myth of the separation of church and state to confine us and distort our doctrine. We've allowed it to suppress God's purpose from the very beginning.

Christians are continually told, "Stay out of governing." We are told over and over again, "You're not intelligent enough to make laws. You don't understand how to govern. Keep your religion within the four walls of your church and be quiet. We will govern and rule. You keep your beliefs out of it." Sadly, a passive, cold church has said, "OK," wrongly thinking God doesn't want us involved in government. A passive church gave up the earth, saying, "We are going to Heaven anyway, so you can have it. We're out of here." An escape mentality became the perspective.

Even though I believe that Jesus is coming and we will be taken out of here at some point, an escape mentality stops us from occupying or taking care of God's business until He comes. We have conveniently suppressed the truth, thus empowering hell's kingdom to rule the nations, territories, and lands in our place. We are giving up our gardens just as surely as Adam and Eve gave up theirs, and it is time for it to stop. All of creation is crying out for it to stop.

It's time to know the truth and let it make us free. It's time to rule and reign with Christ in this life, governing by declaring, cultivating, and making a stand for God's Word. As heirs of God and joint heirs with Christ, we are to subdue the earth and exercise dominion.

It's time for the New Testament church and remnant believers to arise and say what God says. That is how we rule. It's time to raise our voices, shake off deadly passivity, and fulfill the dominion mandate God has given us. Each of us should be planting God's Word into our nation, sowing it into our societies, declaring it into all seven realms of society—education, business, government, media, arts, entertainment, religion, and family.

We need more sons and daughters of God running for political office—those with a biblical worldview that they will not compromise. It's time for the rest of us to back them and rule as originally intended. The world is meant to be discipled by the sons and daughters of God who realize and use their authority in Jesus' name.

THE GREAT COMMISSION

And Jesus came and spoke to them, saying, "All authority has been given to Me in heaven and on earth. Go therefore and make disciples of all the nations, baptizing them in the name of the Father and of the Son and of the Holy Spirit, teaching them to observe all things that I have commanded you; and lo, I am with you always, even to the end of the age" (Matthew 28:18-20 NKJV).

Jesus said to make disciples of all the nations, teaching them His commands. Most believers today read that with a worldview that suppresses truth. They read it as, "Go and win souls for Christ." And, of course, we should. I believe that, and I have preached that for 37 years. We should disciple as many people as we possibly can. Jesus discipled twelve, then seventy, and then many more. But don't suppress what He says or change His words. Go make disciples of all *nations*. It is a command of King Jesus, a scriptural commissioning, and God has purposed and Christ has commissioned believers to disciple nations.

Where can you see "stay out of government" in any of what Jesus said? Stay out of law making. Stay separate from the state. Don't involve your religion in government. Don't rule. Don't get involved in societal issues. It's certainly not what the Bible says. God says to be involved in government. He says it in the Old and the New Testament. He doesn't change it. It is a doctrine of demons that tells us to stay out of earth's government, and we are seeing this in our nation because we have not understood and done what God says.

We cannot disciple a nation without being involved. It just can't be done. When you buy into the lie of separation of church and state, you empower liars every time. The church in the past few decades has been doing exactly that—empowering liars. I know that's tough to hear, but I also know it's the truth. We have got to wake up and start tending the garden. We've got to disciple this nation.

The word for "nation" in the Greek is *ethnos,* and it means tribes, clans, races that share the same habitat, territory, land, or country (Strong, G1484). A nation is a territory of people who have things in common with each other—always location, usually language, sometimes ethnicity. For example, Germanic people congregate in Germany where they speak German. I know that's heavy revelation, but that's what happens. There's a nation of them. Once upon a time, a certain ethnic group settled there. Likewise, France is filled with certain races of people who shared and settled that territory and became the French. The point is, God cares about our social connectedness, our cultural and racial backgrounds, and our places of origin because these things are part of our identity and they clarify some of our purpose. He cares about how we function together in earth societies, about laws promoting justice and righteousness within those connected societies, and He cares about the decisions that affect us all.

Politics is the realm where decisions and laws that govern a nation are made. It sets the atmosphere and the parameters for a populace to live in. Those who set the language of society control the society. It's politics. We are not to stay out of that conversation. We are to be a voice, strong for our God. Our words, our declarations, our decrees, and our stand for truth are to set the parameters and the atmosphere for the populace. This is our mandate. We have been commissioned by our King, and yet millions in the church don't even know it and are perishing for lack of knowledge.

We are not just commissioned to disciple as many people as we possibly can; we are also called to disciple their governance. God says we are to set the atmosphere and the parameters for good societal living. It's not either; it's both. We are to teach them what Christ says, not our ideas or opinions. We are not to give them the balanced perspective of Buddha, Mohammad, or Confucius. To disciple, we must declare what God says and engage in governing issues and laws accordingly. We are planting God's Kingdom, setting it, laying its foundation, and never backing off.

We've got to engage in politics. We cannot disciple if we are silent. Passive silence gives voice to liars and enables demon doctrines to prevail and penetrate our nation, our culture, and our societies.

We are called to declare the truth, and our King says, "If you will declare the truth, that is what will be done. It will produce after its kind. It will prevail." The majority of the church has embraced the myths and distortions of demon doctrine. That twisted truth told us to stay out of government, when all along God wanted us to stay involved.

When God's people stand for biblical principles, it produces righteousness that exalts a nation. Suppressing those principles through silent surrender results in foolishness. It darkens hearts and minds and causes chaos. Who could deny that's happening today? Suppression leaves a void and empowers fools, allowing demons to rule. It hands authority over to demons.

We are in desperate need today for true disciples of Christ to arise and disciple this nation, to speak the Word of God no matter what into every level of society. It is a lie to say it's not God's plan that we get involved in social, political, or governmental issues or law. It's been His plan since day one, and it was still His plan when Jesus rose from the dead saying, "Go make disciples of all nations." It's a primary purpose of His church, and millions are dammed because the church has not done it.

"I am giving you authority." What a statement! "Go make a stand for what I said." It is high time that we do it. The coming generation is perishing before our eyes because they lack God's perspective of reality. Listen to them—they make no sense. Listen to government—it makes no sense. I mean, how many times have I almost thrown something at my television over this nonsense? That is the definition of foolishness. It's time for us to fulfill the mandate. It's time for the sons and daughters of God to step up, make a stand, and stop the politically correct compromise. It's time to plant the Word of God into every level of society and let the chips fall wherever they fall. It doesn't make any difference what they call us. It makes all the difference to me what God calls us.

The dominion mandate is a message of truth that must be restored to the Body of Christ. While the whole world may not see it, the remnant will see it. This means that if you are a son or a daughter of God, He has restored His original intent for you and you are to enforce it. It could be through assisting someone else, raising your voice, making a stand somewhere, or through financial means. It's time for us to embrace the responsibility. It's time to butt heads with those who say, "Be quiet." No, I will not be quiet. I am God's son. I am God's daughter. I am here to declare what He says.

THE REIGNING CHURCH, CHRIST'S EKKLESIA

When Jesus came into the coasts of Caesarea Philippi, he
asked his disciples, saying, Whom do men say that I the
Son of man am? And they said, Some say that thou art John
the Baptist: some, Elias; and others, Jeremias, or one of the
prophets. He saith unto them, But whom say ye that I am?
And Simon Peter answered and said, Thou art the Christ,
the Son of the living God. And Jesus answered and said
unto him, Blessed art thou, Simon Barjona: for flesh and
blood hath not revealed it unto thee, but my Father which
is in heaven. And I say also unto thee, That thou art Peter,
and upon this rock I will build my church; and the gates of
hell shall not prevail against it. And I will give unto thee the
keys of the kingdom of heaven: and whatsoever thou shalt
bind on earth shall be bound in heaven: and whatsoever
thou shalt loose on earth shall be loosed in heaven.
—MATTHEW 16:13-19

As sons and daughters of God, we are commanded to forbid or
to permit things on earth. God's original intent for His people is to

reign with Him and exercise dominion, declaring God's Word into the nations. God's purpose for the church is for it to be involved in government. It is vitally important to see the church in context with Jesus Himself. That context is a King and His Kingdom.

Understand, please, that Jesus does not talk about His church first. He establishes His Kingdom first. He does that for nearly three years, and then at the very end of His ministry He mentions the church. You would think He would start off talking about His church, but He doesn't. John the Baptist and the disciples all preached the Gospel of the Kingdom. They preached, saying, "Repent, for the Kingdom of Heaven is at hand." It is near you. It is here right now.

UNDERSTANDING KINGDOM

Jesus came to start a Kingdom that Isaiah said would have no end. A quick review of the Book of Matthew highlights the overwhelming importance the Godhead placed upon this. It's why Jesus didn't start explaining His church first. You cannot understand what real church is until you understand Kingdom. The church is a part of His Kingdom. The world right now is in an absolute mess because we have not understood that the church is to be a ruling and reigning branch of His Kingdom upon the earth. In fact, Kingdom has been minimized by the nominal (in name only) church in our times. Christ's intent that His church should rule and reign has been completely distorted. Most believers have been taught the exact opposite. I was raised in church and I was taught the exact opposite. Hell has worked for centuries to suppress this truth, and yes, satan has even used the church to suppress this truth.

The message of the Kingdom today and the ruling and reigning mandate upon the church has been put off into the future. We need to see what Jesus says. I am more interested in what Jesus says than what man, the devil, or our government says. It seems to me to be common sense that Jesus would define what He means by the church that He is building. He did say, *"I will build my church; and the gates of hell shall not prevail against it."* Why would we allow anyone else but Jesus Himself to define what He means? That makes no sense to me. What He meant is a bit complicated, but it's not hard to understand if we have the right definitions. It's been clouded up because of man's ideas that have gotten in the way of the truth.

The answer to all the chaos and confusion in our world today is the church rising up to be what Christ says the church is to be. It is abundantly clear to anyone who will take an honest look at Scripture that Jesus came to start a Kingdom. He came to build a spiritual Kingdom that would represent Him on the earth, a spiritual Kingdom that would visibly affect the earth.

When you think about a spiritual Kingdom, do not think *unreal*— think *real but unseen*. For example, while you can't see Heaven right now, decisions made in Heaven can and do affect things on the earth. Christ's Kingdom is a spiritual Kingdom that does visibly affect the world, even though it's invisible to the natural eye. It is a real Kingdom. It is not a phantom Kingdom, nor is it one that is off in the future somewhere as most today describe it.

A KINGDOM WORLDVIEW

Jesus Christ came teaching the reality of the Kingdom because He wanted this truth to be the worldview of His sons and daughters. If we don't understand this, Christianity does not work as originally intended, at least not to its fullest extent. The dominion mandate and the great commission to go into all the world and disciple nations will not happen without a Kingdom worldview. That's why Lucifer and his powers fight the message of the Kingdom so hard. He doesn't want us reigning with Christ in this life. He doesn't want us exercising dominion. He doesn't want us to understand what Jesus originally meant. He wants us to be ignorant and passive.

Jesus did not come to start a Kingdom that would be dormant for 2,000 years. That would make no sense. He expects His Kingdom to rule and reign with Him on this earth right now. Through prayer decrees and planting God's word seeds, He expects His joint heirs to keep good foundations maintained upon the earth so that government can be built on a solid social structure. He expects them to, in His name, forbid some things and permit some things. He expects His influence to enter into a culture and change that culture through His born-again ones teaching exactly what He says. He expects His church to act like it's supposed to act and to work for what His Word says must be accomplished.

KINGDOM

The word for "kingdom" is the Greek word *basileia* meaning royal dominion, to rule, the realm of a king, and a kingdom's reign (Strong, G932). The English word is composed of two other words—*king* and *-dom*, a suffix meaning "domain." A *king's domain* is his kingdom. A kingdom is a government that rules a territory, an area, or a nation. The Scriptures teach emphatically that Jesus is a King, He has a Kingdom, and He rules a territory. Naturally, His rule is boundless. His domain is everywhere—in heaven and upon the earth. He even rules hell itself because He has the keys, which represent authority.

Jesus being King of Heaven is not argued very much among Christians. But that He is King over the earth is often dispensationalized. It's put off into the future as though the earth is not yet a part of His domain or jurisdiction, which is exactly wrong. To say that would limit His authority, and you can't do that because Jesus Himself said, *"All authority has been given to Me in heaven and on earth"* (Matt. 28:18 NKJV). He spoke that word in the present tense, so that must mean that He is King of Heaven and He is King of earth right now. He is sovereign over it all right now.

How does that work? It's supposed to work through His Kingdom's church, which is His body (see Eph. 1:23). The church is to be Christ's ruling body on the earth. Remember from Romans 8:17, we are *"heirs of God, and joint-heirs with Christ."* We are identical heirs with Christ right now, and in His name we are to rule on the earth. Yes, we are going to rule with Him through eternity, but we need to reign with Him now as well. We should not dispensationalize it away into the future.

JESUS PREACHED KINGDOM

Christ declared the Kingdom before he ever introduced His church. I think most would agree that His very first sermon was a sermon that He thought through very carefully. Jesus is brilliant. He is a genius. No one can communicate like Him. No one ever spoke like He spoke. No doubt His first sermon was designed with a very clear purpose. It's found in Matthew 4:23-24:

> *Jesus traveled throughout the region of Galilee, teaching in the synagogues and announcing the Good News about the Kingdom. And he healed every kind of disease and illness. News about him spread as far as Syria, and people soon began bringing to him all who were sick. And whatever their sickness or disease, or if they were demon possessed or epileptic or paralyzed—he healed them all* (NLT).

Notice He preached the Gospel of the Kingdom and He never stopped preaching the Kingdom. Moffatt's translation reads, *"He made a tour through the whole of Galilee...preaching the gospel of the Reign."* The church has preached many things—it preaches most of the things found in the Bible—but it has not preached the Gospel of the reign, the rule, or the governing. Jesus preached the Sermon on the Mount, beginning with Matthew 5:3 (NLT), saying, *"God blesses those who are poor and realize their need for him, for the Kingdom of Heaven is theirs,"* and ending that with verse 10, saying, *"God blesses those who are persecuted for doing right, for the Kingdom of Heaven is theirs"* (NLT). He begins and He ends with the good news of the Kingdom.

In chapter 6 of Matthew, He preaches on prayer, saying, *"In this manner, therefore, pray: Our Father in heaven, hallowed be Your name. Your kingdom come. Your will be done on earth as it is in heaven"* (Matt. 6:9-10 NKJV). The Greek speaks that in a declarative way. In other words, He said, "Kingdom, come." That's what we are to declare. "Kingdom, come to our region. Kingdom of God, come and reign over this territory."

Then Christ preaches in Matthew 7:12 what we simply call the Golden Rule, "Do unto others as you would have others do unto you." He says, *"You can enter God's Kingdom only through the narrow gate. The highway to hell is broad, and its gate is wide for the many who choose that way. But the gateway to life is very narrow and the road is difficult, and only a few ever find it"* (Matt. 7:13-14 NLT). The Kingdom way is a narrow way. He is not talking about something off in the future. He is talking about the Kingdom way right now.

> *Not all people who sound religious are really godly. They may refer to me as "Lord," but they still won't enter the Kingdom of Heaven. The decisive issue is whether they obey my Father in heaven. On judgment day many will tell me, "Lord, Lord, we prophesied in your name and cast out demons in your name and performed many miracles in your name." But I will reply, "I never knew you, go away; the things you did were unauthorized"* (Matthew 7:21-23 NLT, 1996 edition).

If you do things that are not authorized, you are apostate and you're sent away from Him. In others words, you are a phony. You can't be a part of His Kingdom and do unauthorized things. You can't ordain homosexuals; it's unauthorized. You can't preach Chrislam; it's unauthorized. You can't say everybody is going to Heaven, no matter what; it's unauthorized. If you can't enter into Heaven and you are sent away, then there is only one other choice—hell. No, not everyone is going to Heaven; our King says so. It's unauthorized to say it, and if you do then the King says, "I will say get away from me. You're not entering the Kingdom of Heaven." You must preach what is authorized and plant the uncompromised Word of the Living God. You can't suppress what it's saying. If you do, He could send you away.

Jesus began His Galilean ministry by preaching in Matthew 9:35, *"And Jesus went about all the cities and villages, teaching in their synagogues, and preaching the gospel of the kingdom, and healing every sickness and every disease among the people."* Why would He be preaching the Gospel of the Kingdom if it was for the future? Especially when He demonstrated that the Kingdom of Heaven was among them by healing the sick and diseased.

Later, Jesus sent His twelve disciples out to preach. He empowered them when they went to cast out devils and to heal the sick. And what were they to preach? In Matthew 10:7 Jesus said, *"And as ye go, preach, saying, The kingdom of heaven is at hand."* It is near you—right at your fingertips. You can touch it. Demonstrate that by casting out demons and healing the sick. The Message Bible reads, *"Tell them that the kingdom is here."* J.B. Phillips' translation says, *"Proclaim that the kingdom of Heaven has arrived."* That doesn't sound like it's off in the future to me.

Christ made these statements 2,000 years ago, so He can't be talking about the future. He said to them, "Declare the Kingdom of God is here now," and then the Book of Matthew continues with one parable after another concerning the Kingdom of God and what the Kingdom of God is like. The point is, Jesus did His very best to get His disciples to understand the Gospel of the Kingdom. He wanted them to think Kingdom. He insisted that they renew their minds to that world-view. Over and over He said that He came to plant a Kingdom on the earth—a Kingdom that cannot be shaken. A Kingdom that He said will never come to an end. So when He begins to speak of the church, without question the context is the Kingdom of God. The church is a part of His Kingdom upon the earth.

CHRIST'S CHURCH

The picture of a kingdom that grows and prospers on the earth is strengthened by the word Jesus chose to refer to His church. After three years of teaching the Kingdom, He used a political, judicial, and governmental word to introduce His church into the earth. That astonishes a lot of people. But remember, God wants His sons and His daughters reigning with Him. We are made in His image and He is a ruler, a governor, and a King, so the nature to govern is planted into our being the day that we are born again. It's a part of our spiritual DNA.

The word Jesus uses for "church" emphatically reflects that. That word is *ekklesia,* and it is translated "church" 113 times in the New Testament (Strong, G1577). Jesus, the disciples, and the apostles used *ekklesia* to describe the church. It is not a religious word. It is not even a sacred word, and in the Bible it never denotes a building or a specific place of worship. Of course, it has come to mean that today. We say, "I am going to church today," or someone may ask, "Where do you go to church?"

Technically, that is not possible because *you are the church.* The word *church* originally meant an assembly of those called out for a purpose. Yes, a part of that purpose is worship, a part of it is teaching, and a part of it is discipline, but those are not the whole purpose, and place is never a factor. You can worship any place. If Christ meant to speak of a place, He would have used the word *synagogue* or *temple*.

The English word *church* does not appear in New Testament translations until 1557 in the Geneva New Testament. That is the first time the word *church* is ever used—1,500 years after Christ. Until then, ekklesia was translated as assembly, congregation, an assembly of called out ones, or specially assembled ones.

The Geneva New Testament was translated in Geneva, Switzerland. The translators were greatly influenced by Theodore Beza and John Calvin, the protestant leaders in Geneva. Beza essentially invented the word *church*, specifically to refer to certain religious orders governed by a hierarchy (such as the Catholic Church or the Puritans). These orders had individual churches all over the world, but one central government that controlled them all through many levels of religious authority. To describe this, Beza used the Greek word *kyridakon* to come up with the English word *church*, but it is never found in the New Testament.

The King of England at the time was King James, a very religious man. He liked the word *church* and was fond of hierarchies (not surprising, as he was a king himself), and in 1611 he ordered that the King James Authorized Version be written with fifteen rules the translators were bound to. One of those rules was that the New Testament Greek word *ekklesia* always be translated with the English word *church*, and that rule stuck in other translations from then on.

Once the word *church* was in place in the English Bible, anyone who read it would read "church" every time the original authors used "ekklesia." Over time, the word *church* gained a broader meaning, evolving to mean a location, a hierarchal religious order, a place of worship, a holy place, or a building. None of these ideas are even close to anything Jesus meant when He spoke of ekklesia.

Notice the distinction between *ekklesia*, an assembly or group of people, and *church*—a location with a building (and probably some people in it). This is subtle, but it is a dangerous confusion that has caused most people today to hear *church* and think place, not Kingdom. Hell's definition confines the most powerful governing body on the earth, the ekklesia, to within the walls of a building on Sunday morning.

Christ never said, "I will build My synagogue or temple, and the gates of hell will not prevail against its walls." He said, "I will build My ekklesia, and the gates of hell will not prevail against them." Knowing who Jesus is and His brilliance, we have to conclude that He did not use this word accidentally to describe His church. It was stated on purpose, it was Godhead planned, and no other word is ever used. It's ekklesia in all four Gospels, in Acts, in Romans, in the Epistles, in Timothy, Titus, Hebrews, and Revelation. It is never another word. We must understand the meaning of ekklesia if we are going to understand what Jesus intended His church to be.

By the way, just so you know, I do love the word *church*. I can't think of another word, and I'm not on a campaign to change it. We need a good English word and church fits, but we've got to understand what it originally meant when Jesus used it. What we call church today He called *ekklesia*. Make no mistake about it—He knew exactly what He was saying and what He meant. The true meaning of ekklesia is so radical that many people are scared to even go there.

EKKLESIA

What does *ekklesia* mean? It is from two Greek words: *ek* and *kaleo*. *Ek* means out and *kaleo* means to call out (Strong, G1537, G2564). It means to be called out and assembled for a purpose. The word ekklesia first occurs in the 5th Century (500 years) before Christ. Again, it was a political term, not a religious term. It is a word describing those with the final say in Greek government. The definition of ekklesia in classical Greek is, *"An assembly of citizens summoned by the town crier to legislative assembly at the gate."* The gate, of course, is where people of authority sat. It would be like where our city building is, where the mayor and the city council do business. The capital of Ohio would be the gate of Ohio. It's where our governor, Senate, and House governs from. Washington, D.C. would be called the gate of the United States in Bible days. Citizens eighteen years of age and up could answer a call to gather or assemble to pass legislation, always by upraised hand.

Colin Brown states in the *New International Dictionary of New Testament Theology* volume 3, "The ekklesia denotes in the usage of antiquity the popular assembly of the competent full citizens of a city. It met at regular intervals but could also be called quickly in cases of emergency." The ekklesia's sphere of competence included:

A. Decisions on suggested law and final decisions on new law.

The final decision of all law was left to the ekklesia. Don't think Jesus didn't know what He was talking about. "My church is to have the final decision on laws in the nation or region." He said it, not me!

B. Appointments to official positions.

Voting was for magistrates or for those who held an office. It was the ekklesia's responsibility to vote for those who held office.

C. Both internal and external policies in the region including contracts, treaties, war and peace, and financial matters for the region.

They were all decided by the ekklesia. It is not conceivable that Jesus didn't know what the word *ekklesia* meant when He used it. He understood it very well.

D. The ekklesia would rule on cases of treason.

If someone was involved in treason, they would be brought before the ekklesia, and they would vote and decide their guilt or innocence.

E. It could summon for its army to assemble for war.

The ekklesia had command of the military, which is certainly a lot of authority.

F. The ekklesia ruled on societal and cultural matters for its geographical location or territory.

Jesus said, "My ekklesia is to set the cultural standards for a region." He understood what it meant.

G. The ekklesia chose by upraised hands who would sit at the Areopagus (the high court of Athens).[1]

The capital of Greece was Athens, the gate of Greece. The high court there was similar to our Supreme Court today. It was the Supreme Court of Athens, Greece.

The *Areopagus* literally means "the Rock of Ares." Athens was a city where the temples of many gods were, and it had cultural facilities that defined the culture of the nation—including the high court. The Areopagus was where the high court of Greece sat to deliberate.

Notice, the ekklesia was not the high court—it was the assembly of the people—but it decided who would be on the high court. Those in the Areopagus were selected by the ekklesia. Both groups had their legal roles, with a nuanced interplay, but from what we can discover the ekklesia remained the final authority. For example, the high court (Areopagus) could investigate corruption or treason, but then the evidence was taken to the ekklesia for sentencing.[2]

Some citizens were required to attend the ekklesia, but many more were not—their presence was voluntary. The decisions of government were up to those who answered the call to assemble and rule. That's why I have taught for years in favor of voting in elections. It is our responsibility, commanded by our King, to be responsible for who sits on the court. Biblically, voting is a responsibility. If you are a Christian, raise your hand and make a decision. Nothing secret. Raise your hand and be seen. Publicly decide.

Also, the Areopagus in Athens was the gateway of Greece where philosophies were debated. Pope John Paul II said that today's media is our modern-day Areopagus. This is very insightful because the people in the media are now the ones who are spinning the new philosophies. The media is now trying to decide who holds official positions and who sits on the Supreme Court. The media promotes godless ways, and it's telling the church to be quiet. They have stolen the authority of the Areopagus, and we can't stand for it.

The apostle Paul was so concerned about the cultural conditions and the idol worship in Athens that he went and preached a sermon at the Areopagus, saying:

> When I arrived here the other day, I was fascinated with all the shrines I came across. And then I found one inscribed, to the god nobody knows. I'm here to introduce you to this God so you can worship intelligently, know who you're dealing with (Acts 17:23 MSG).

In ancient Greek terms, he preached a sermon about Jesus Christ at the Supreme Court. The apostle Paul did not stay out of the judicial system. He exercised his God-given authority to speak into it. He raised his hand. He said, "Let me tell you about this unknown God. Let me tell you that the philosophies that you are spinning are godless. Let me encourage you to change your ways." He preached a message at the high court calling them out for their godless laws. It's probably why he got beat up, but he did it.

A GOVERNING BODY

We need to understand the kind of authority an ekklesia held in order to fully grasp what Jesus meant when He used the word. "When the Greek city-states found their governments had become too corrupt and oppressive, they would call for an *ekklesia*, an assembly outside the civil authority of the city. If enough people came out and refused to accept the existing centralized civil authority, that government would collapse."[3] Due to the ekklesia's authority, civil leaders could be replaced to ensure the ekklesia's rule was enforced. Wow. That's pretty strong authority. Remember, Jesus said His ekklesia would forbid some things and permit some things. There are some people we should forbid from holding office. There are others we should permit.

Thayer's Greek Lexicon defines *ekklesia* as "an assembly of people convened at the public place of council for the purpose of deliberating." *Deliberating* means thinking through things very carefully. The ekklesia is to think through cultural standards and then raise their voice by voting on those standards. It is not biblical to not vote. Godless politicians have been placed into office because believers sit at home and don't vote.

The Romans, who were the governing power when Christ made the statement in Matthew 16:18, also had ekklesias. Don't think Jesus didn't know it. He knew it very well. When Rome would conquer a territory they would send in a group of administrators, legislators, or regulators of culture. How did they regulate?

- They regulated by shaping the culture. "Here is what the culture is going to be allowed to do."

- They shaped the education system of the region. "Here is what you will teach."

- They administered laws, societal standards, and taxes.

The idea was to make that province look like Rome, reform it to be a little Rome, and make it compatible with Roman rule. They called that governing council the ekklesia. The Jewish people were under a Roman ekklesia too. Don't think Jesus didn't realize that.

Now we have a more complete context for what Jesus is saying. We see what *ekklesia* meant at the time, and we see that the first mention of church is within the context of the Kingdom of God. So the contextual definition is this: "The Kingdom of God's governing, ruling body is the ekklesia, established by King Jesus to look after His Kingdom on earth." We have to get that. The ruling Kingdom is not for a future time in Heaven because it won't be necessary there.

Every kingdom has six distinct areas that bring identity to it:

1. A king—ours is Jesus and we have no other king but Jesus.

2. Geographical boundaries—our kingdom does also; it's everywhere.

3 Laws and commands—our constitution is the Word of Almighty God. It is the Bible.

4. A society or culture that shapes it—ours is in our hearts, transmitted there by Holy Spirit who governs our conscience.

5. A political government—it legislates and has standards it maintains. If you are part of any Christian effort that has no standards, it is not part of His Kingdom

6. An economy—ours is called tithes and offerings. Ten percent.

Jesus said, "The body who stewards this for Me is My church, My ekklesia, My called-out ones. The born-again citizens of My Kingdom will worship Me as their King, represent Me as their King, and in My name they will steward their territorial or geographical boundaries. They will steward the laws and commands to ensure they are biblically based. They will steward societal and cultural values to conform to and be shaped by My ways and Word. They will call to account political governments. They will decide official positions and remove some from official positions by voting. Some have got to go. It's the church's responsibility. They will, in My name, steward economies, insisting on ethical financial behavior by voting over what is acceptable."

Apostle Joseph Mattera writes that by using the word *ekklesia*, "Jesus called His followers the new congress of His kingdom."[4] That's the best definition I've seen yet. Jesus says believers are to come together and they are to rule with Him in His name on the earth. Where in the world can you possibly find separation of church and state in any of that? We have fallen so far short of what Jesus meant by "church" that it is embarrassing. We have wrongly bought the idea that we are to stay out of politics, legislation, and cultural decisions when, in fact, the very word for *church* in Scripture is a political word—a ruling body, a governing body, a legislative body. It is a congress, and make no mistake—Jesus knew exactly what that was.

Read this testimony from a personal friend of ours.

CANDICE'S STORY

As CEO of a pro-life agency, I often dream that I am rescuing babies. From accidents, from animals, from predators. It's a residual effect of the work we do. The cause permeates your very being and you struggle with how to accomplish more.

In 2015, as I watched the Heartbeat Bill lay dead in the Ohio Senate for the fifth straight year, I wondered who would ever rise up to speak for the innocent unborn. We had a conservative majority, and yet supposed pro-life members were not bold enough to protect an unborn child whose heart could be heard beating?

One night, I had a dream of a different kind. It was only a voice saying, "Whom shall I send, and who will go for us? Then said I, Here am I; send me" (Isaiah 6:8). The word "us" ripped at my heart. Sixty million babies have died and their voices have never been heard.

In my own life, God has always made me do the thing of which I am most afraid. Looking back, I see how God was with me, preparing me all my life. He equipped me, even when I did not realize it.

A vacant seat was upcoming in our local House race and my husband and I decided that I should try to win the seat. I had never run for public office and it was a long shot. I knew I would be defined as a "one-issue candidate." When we filed to run, we were immediately attacked from all sides but we kept our eyes on the finish line.

Much to our shock, the church began to mobilize on my behalf. Both evangelicals and Catholics took my pro-life stance to heart and they formed a formidable volunteer base of over 1,000 workers. I ran against a person with strong name recognition and good financial backing. In fact, I was outspent nearly two to one.

On primary day, we went home exhausted after weeks of nonstop campaigning and watched the returns roll across the bottom of our television screen. I won with nearly

60 percent of the vote and I will leave for the Ohio State-house in just a few days.

"God is preparing His heroes and when the opportunity comes, He can fit them into their places in a moment. And the world will wonder where they came from." —A.B. Simpson

I am only one person but I have an army behind me. We must be willing to risk it all. If we lose, we lose. But we must fight. There is no other way. This is the thing the enemy fears the most. —Candice Keller, State Representative, Ohio's 53rd House District

By using the word *ekklesia* Jesus was clearly saying, "Church, get involved and shape your culture. If it is wrong, don't hide. Raise your hand. Be vocal. Be public and forbid it. Rebuke things in My name. Forbid some things in My name and permit what is biblical. Affect public policy. Make sure you have the final say. Make the final choice. Get involved in the laws of your land. Get involved in matters of war and treaties. Speak up against corruption. Don't be passive and say nothing. If it's corrupt, say so. Vote it gone. Rule against it in My name. Only back those in any kind of official capacity who will obey My Word."

"Ekklesia, church, speak up against adultery in your capital, your gates. Rule against ridiculous philosophies that are coming out of your capitals and ideas or philosophies that justify sin and pollute the culture. Speak up and raise your hand. Vote and rule against it. You're My legislative body on the planet. You're My congress. Regulate the laws of your land. Regulate the culture you are going to live in. Say no to social corruption. Transform your territories. Shape them to look like a little bit of Heaven on earth. Shape the culture you are living in. Decide societal issues. Decide the economy. Decide tax issues, and only back those who honor the Word of God."

Remember, the prophet Samuel told King Saul, "Do not take any of the spoils of war. You kill every animal, all the goats; you don't take any of it" (see 1 Sam. 15). But King Saul did. He kept the animals for himself, and what did Samuel do? He stepped up and said, "The Lord now rejects you from being king." He ruled against him. He said that he was no longer permitted to be the king of Israel and he began to work to overthrow him and he did. Saul's government did not prevail. The Kingdom of God did prevail and David took his place. There are times when we have to say, "That is it. You are rejected from being a leader over us."

Christ says to believers, "You may not be the judge who sits on the bench, but you make sure you decide who it is." Make sure you decide who it is by publicly voting on it. Be vocal. You're God's ruling body, so act on it. The world has said repeatedly, "Church, you stay out of politics." They are going to say it more and more through today's media. But Jesus says, "Church, get involved in politics. You're an ekklesia. You're on earth to be My congress."

In our times, the church has misplaced this teaching. We have missed the cultural mandate of our King. We've allowed hell to steal it from us, and we've allowed humanism and the secular church to redefine us. It is time to stop the heresy. It is time for some of us to raise our hands and declare the truth no matter who likes it or who doesn't like it.

The cultural mandate of the Scriptures is that the church is called to be the moral center of the culture and the backbone of its laws by influencing every discipline and jurisdiction with a biblical worldview. It's time we were about the business of doing it and quit apologizing for it. It's time to be what Christ Jesus says we are—an ekklesia raising our hands to affect public policy, judge corruption, pass and enforce legislation that lines up with God's Word, shape the culture, speak against idolatry and vain philosophies, and speak against judges who legislate unrighteousness. We have been authorized in Jesus' name. We have been called to that purpose.

I know that we will never have a utopia upon this planet until Jesus comes back. But we can affect the world and its governments, and we are expected to.

NOTES

1. The quote and seven defining aspects of the ekklesia are taken from Colin Brown, *The New International Dictionary of New Testament Theology*, vol. 3 (Grand Rapids, MI: Zondervan Pub. House, 1975). The comments on each point are the author's.

2. Gustav Gilbert, *The Constitutional Antiquities of Sparta and Athens* (Chicago: Argonaut, 1968) 137–138, 167–168, 265–310.

3. "The Church, the Ekklesia," His Holy Church, March 18, 2015, http://www.hisholychurch.net/ekklesia.php.

4. Joseph Mattera, "God, Politics & the Kingdom of God," Mattera Ministries International, May 13, 2016, Ecclesia, http://josephmattera.org/god-politics-the-kingdom-of-god/.

CHAPTER
5

DECREE YOUR AUTHORITY

If we are going to plant the heavens and lay God's Word into our culture's foundations, we must learn, practice, and activate authority language. The King's seed that is sown into us, the King's DNA that has been transmitted into our spirit at the new birth, needs to manifest inside of us. We need to become who and what we really are. We are under the Lordship of King Jesus, forgiven, re-imaged, and born again into His family. We truly are in the King's lineage. We are heirs of God and we are joint heirs with Christ. We are a part of the Kingdom of Almighty God and are expected to reign with Him right now.

As part of His family, we need to engage in releasing words of power, might, and dominion. If we are going to see things change, we must restore kingly speech and authority language to the Body of Christ. It's time to decree our Kingdom authority, to rise up and rule in this life as intended. It's time to fill and occupy the earth, subduing it and exercising dominion. We should be advancing into positions of authority as the Holy Spirit leads. Some in the Body of Christ are called to positions of governmental authority in the natural realm. If that is you, run toward that and not away from it.

The apostle John speaks of God's intent in Revelation 5:9-10, saying this:

> *And they sung a new song, saying, Thou art worthy to take the book, and to open the seals thereof: for thou wast slain, and hast redeemed us to God by thy blood out of every kindred, and tongue, and people, and nation; and hast made us unto our God kings and priests: and we shall reign on the earth.*

Certainly the fullness of this will occur after Jesus returns to earth Himself, but we are also called to represent His Kingdom now. Jesus said the Kingdom is here; it is at hand. He sent His men out to preach and tell others the Kingdom had arrived. We are to declare this message with authority.

Jesus said, "*I will give you the keys of the kingdom of heaven, and whatever you bind on earth will be bound in heaven, and whatever you loose on earth will be loosed in heaven*" (Matt. 16:19 NKJV). Using the original Greek word meanings, it says this, "Whatever you at any time encounter of hell's council or authority that I am determined My church will prevail against, you will then face the decision whether you will or will not bind it. What transpires is conditional to your response. If you do purposely and consciously involve yourself in binding the issue on earth, you will find at that future moment when you do that it has been yes'd in Heaven." If we say yes, it's been yes'd in Heaven, and if we say no, it's been no'd in Heaven. In other words, the authority He has delegated to us is backed up in Heaven.

KEYS

Keys represent authority in Scripture. If you have the keys to something, you have authority over it. You can open it, or you can close it. We have been given authority in Christ's name to open doors or close doors. We have been given authority to bind things or to loose things. We have the authority to forbid or permit. This authority has been handed to His ekklesia.

In Matthew 16:18-19 (MSG) Jesus said:

> This is the rock on which I will put together my church, a church so expansive with energy that not even the gates of hell will be able to keep it out. "And that's not all. You will have complete and free access to God's kingdom, keys to open any and every door: no more barriers between heaven and earth, earth and heaven. A yes on earth is yes in heaven. A no on earth is no in heaven.

That's an incredible statement. The church that does this is a glorious church. It's time we answer the commissioning of King Jesus and confidently release authority language on the earth. As Job said, "Thou shalt also decree a thing, and it shall be established unto thee" (Job 22:28).

We are not here to be ruled by unrighteousness. That makes no sense. Why would God put us here to be ruled by unrighteousness? We have been legally established as governors, ruling ones given authority by our God. We are heirs now, and we are to declare the uncompromised Word of King Jesus on the earth. We are not to compromise it. We are not to make it politically correct. We are to say what He says.

SPEAKING WITH AUTHORITY

The best example that we have for speaking authority language is, of course, Jesus Himself. John 7:46 says concerning Jesus, "Never a man spake like this man." Matthew 7:28 says, "People were astonished at his doctrine: for he taught them as one having authority." In other words, He spoke differently. His language was powerful and His words were weighty. His sentences were not filled with unbelief. He didn't con-tradict Himself, saying one thing one minute and something else the next. His speech was not confusing. His words were positive, sure, decisive, confident, and bold. He spoke kingly language. For exam-ple, He didn't say to the leper who came asking to be made clean, "I'm not really feeling it today, but I guess I could try." No, He spoke with authority.

In Luke 7, Jesus approached a widow woman who had just lost her only son and was leading a funeral procession right toward Him. Rather than just getting out of the way and letting death walk right by Him, He confronted the situation as Holy Spirit led him. He spoke with authority to the young man, "Rise," and he got up.

In John 9, he didn't tell a man who was born blind, "Blindness is too hard for Me to heal." No, He spoke with authority, and vision came into those blind eyes. In John 11, Jesus didn't tell Lazarus' sisters Mary and Martha, "Sorry about your brother, but there's nothing I can do. He's been in the grave way too long." No, compassion and the energy of the Holy Spirit rose inside of Him, and when it did He spoke with bold authority, "Lazarus, come forth," and he came back to life.

Absolutely no one spoke with more authority than Jesus. He exemplified to His joint heirs the importance of using authority lan-guage. Luke the physician writes in Luke 4:32, *"They were astonished at his doctrine: for his word was with power."* The Amplified Bible, Clas-sic Edition says, *"They were amazed at His teaching, for His word was with authority and ability and weight and power."*

The word for "power" there is *exousia*, the Greek word for author-ity. It means authority, force, forceful, competence, strength, and influence (Strong, G1849). It denotes right and might. It refers to a potentate who rules a territory or a magistrate's jurisdictions. Greek scholar Spiros Zodhiates defines *exousia* as, "To speak as one in control or to speak as one who has the right to do something."

Jesus talked as though He was authorized. He used His words to influence. The words of our King were forceful. He spoke like a potentate. He spoke like a magistrate who knew His jurisdiction. He spoke with power. His words were sure and spoken with might.

In Luke 4:36 (NKJV) it says, *"Then they were all amazed and spoke among themselves, saying, 'What a word this is! For with authority and power He commands the unclean spirits, and they come out.'"* Our King spoke against demon powers and ruled over them. He gave commands to demons. He didn't take commands. He activated His authority with His words, and like a master magistrate He told devils to go and they did. Shouldn't we do likewise? Shouldn't His church do likewise? Shouldn't His heirs' speech drip with authority? Are we not supposed to represent Him? Aren't we to do what He did?

Kings talk differently. Their speech resonates with authority. They carry themselves with authority. It's time for a remnant Bride to begin to carry herself with authority, knowing that a yes on earth is a yes in heaven and a no on earth is a no in heaven. Knowing that Heaven, Holy Spirit, and angel armies are backing it up.

LIVING WORDS

In Mark 13:31, Jesus said, *"Heaven and earth shall pass away: but my words shall not pass away."* He said, "My words are different. They are powerful and energized with authority to produce. My words cause dynamic effects. I use my words to rule and reign in this life on the earth. You're joint heirs with Me; you do the same thing" (see Rom. 8:17). He said in John 6:63, *"It is the spirit that quickeneth; the flesh profiteth nothing: the words that I speak unto you, they are spirit, and they are life."*

Jesus spoke spirit words that are alive and powerful, words quick-ened by the Holy Spirit. To represent our King and our Kingdom, we must learn to speak kingly language. We have to speak strong, force-ful, confident words that are powerful and effective. We cannot give an uncertain sound and reign with Him on the earth. We've got to speak words that rulers and magistrates speak. Knowing our author-ity, it's time to speak with authority. We must plant God's words into the heavens and the earth. They will activate and germinate. They will produce after their kind. They will produce what they are.

To represent Jesus, we must talk like Him. We are to release com-manding words of power and authority against demon powers that rise against us. Knowing who we are, we are to exercise Kingdom jurisdiction in our region. We are to live, move, act, and talk like kings under King Jesus. We're to speak words in His name that are alive, active, and powerful. They are words based upon God's Word, His covenant, His laws, and His principles. We're to activate our authority with our words—the world needs it badly right now.

Sadly, we have embraced the language of sheep rather than the language of kings. Yes, like sheep we follow our great Shepherd Jesus, listening for His voice. We go where He leads. We follow no one else and submit to no one else. But our language is to be the language of kings as we reign with Him like kings and priests. It's time we discern what the Spirit of God is really saying. We do not bow sheepishly to an ungodly world. We do not say "baaaa" to demons. We say, "Go in the name of Jesus Christ." We say, "Be bound by superior forces of the Kingdom of Almighty God in Jesus' name." We say, "We will decide what is done on earth, not you." We do not sheepishly bow to the gates of hell.

We cannot represent a King who spoke with power with wimpy, reticent words from doubtful minds. We cannot represent Him with negative statements from intimidated thinking. We cannot stand in the face of demons from hell and speak quiet, shy words of compromise. We cannot sheepishly run from the gates or the authorities of hell. We cannot speak fearful, timorous words of trepidation that grovel around in cringing weakness because of our cowardice.

We cannot gaze silently and then just slink away in spineless apprehension like slaves rather than kings. We can't speak dispirited, lifeless words of human doctrine. We can't declare His doctrine in power and ours in impotence. He cannot speak living words of faith and we speak dead words of doubt. We cannot feebly declare the Kingdom of Heaven is here. No—if it's here, we need to declare it with power and authority language.

THE APOSTLES' PRAYER

Kings speak with authority. To be kings and priests of His household who rule and reign with Him in this life, we are going to have to do it with some boldness. We must declare the Word of God with authority. The early church understood this, and we need to understand it also. The prophets and apostles in the Book of Acts operated in very bold authority. They spoke the king's language. In fact, the apostles' prayer shows their awareness of it.

> Grant unto thy servants, that with all boldness they may speak thy word, by stretching forth thine hand to heal; and that signs and wonders may be done by the name of thy holy child Jesus. And when they had prayed, the place was shaken where they were assembled together; and they were all filled with the Holy Ghost, and they spake the word of God with boldness (Acts 4:29-31).

The apostles' prayer needs to become a prayer for today's church. Notice, they were all filled with the Holy Spirit, and they all spoke the Word of God with boldness. That needs to happen today. The apostles and the saints together form an authoritative voice—a voice that represents the King. "Boldness" in these verses is the Greek word *parrhesia,* meaning outspokenness, frankness, commanding words, and commands (Strong, G3954). It is actually a military word concerning leaders or generals. Generals are commanders. They are given command of troops. Why? Because they make commands. *Parrhesia.* We are commanding ones.

Parrhesia means freedom to say or command and confidence to say. Obviously, we are to say some things. We are to be outspoken. *Parrhesia* is a combination of two words—*pas* and *rheo. Pas* means the way or manner, and *rheo* means speak, command, or say (Strong, G3956, G4483). In other words, they understood the way or the manner they spoke was important. They understood that how they talked mattered. "Grant us boldness to make king commands. Give us freedom to be outspoken for our King. Give us confidence to say what He says. Give us boldness to command healings and miracles in the name of Jesus. As kings under Christ's command, anoint us to talk like household kings, like generals giving authoritative commands. Anoint us to rule like kings in this life, giving us boldness to live out our lives like God's kids."

God took a people who dared to pray that prayer and He anointed them to reign with Him. He confirmed their bold faith commands with signs, wonders, and miracles. He gave them harvest after harvest after harvest until harvests were no longer added to them—they were multiplied to them. Their influence turned the world upside down. Today's church is being reintroduced to a revelation that is indeed revolutionary.

Because of the subtle suppression and distortion of truth by our adversaries; because of humanistic doctrine from man that has penetrated the church today; because of pharisaical laws that have a form of godliness but deny the power thereof; and because of religious spirits that want to rule in place of God, this truth concerning authority language has been dormant now for centuries. But Holy Spirit is quickening it yet again. Holy Spirit is anointing this truth to be heard for such a time as this. He is breathing life on this word and upon those who will hear it.

The ekklesia is going to rise up and become the King's voice upon this earth again. The King's voice is going to fill their lips. The church is rising from the ash heaps of religious bondage. It is rising from the desolation of pharisaical laws. His ekklesia is rising in spite of critical spirits designed to muzzle God's people. It is rising in spite of political pressure and even societal pressure to keep silent. His born-again ones are rising in spite of politically correct language that is intolerant and even despises those who will stand for something.

The King's kids in His church are starting to find their voice. The saints are rising to a new level of authority because Christ the King will have a strong, clear, powerful, bold voice on the earth. He will be represented accurately and well.

We need to pray with authority language. We need to speak with authority language. We need to decree our faith with authority language. We need to say what God says with authority language.

It is time to release authority language into your atmosphere. Until it's decreed, the seed is dormant. It's time to plant the heavens. It's time to plant the earth. It's time to decree what God says. What God says matters and it will work. God is on our side. He said, "A *no* on earth is a *no* in Heaven if you will boldly say it in My name, and a *yes* on earth is a *yes* in Heaven. What do you want, a *yes* or a *no*? I am delegating it to you."

Exercise your God-given authority and begin decreeing today, "Father, because we are joint heirs with Jesus, in His name we rise to plant the heavens and the earth with faith decrees aligned with Your Word."

DECREES

WE DECREE EVERY PROMISE OF GOD IS OURS IN JESUS' NAME.

"Lord, You made so many promises to us, one after another after another. We declare every one of them is coming to fullness right now in the name of Jesus. Every good and precious promise of God is coming alive and is now working in our lives. We believe the promises of the Almighty God that you have made to us for decades now. One after the other after the other. Life them in Jesus' name. We declare them to come alive and live among us."

WE DECREE COVENANT BLESSINGS ARE WORKING IN THE LIVES OF GOD'S PEOPLE RIGHT HERE AND RIGHT NOW.

"Covenant blessings are active in our homes. We declare Your covenants, laws, and words are planted into our lives. We plant them into our city. We plant them into our region, our state, and our nation. Your rule of law, your covenants, and your Word. We lay them as a foundation in Jesus' name, and we declare, Lord, give us those who will honor Your Word in governmental positions. Give us political leaders, governors, mayors, everyone who leads or steps to the forefront in an official position, give us those who will honor Your Word. We speak against those who will not. Remove them in the name of Jesus. We would dare do as Your Word says, forbidding them from leading us. We will not be led by unrighteousness."

WE DECREE MIRACLES ARE BEING RELEASED TODAY IN JESUS' NAME.

"Any obstacles of delay, we bind you in the name of Jesus Christ. You stop it and you get out of the way. We declare the wonders of Heaven will be seen. Loose them, Lord. Amazing signs, unfold now. Irrefutable signs, bringing focus on a living, awesome, true God."

WE DECREE OUR CHURCHES ARE BEING FILLED WITH THE PRESENCE OF KING JESUS, HIS HOLY SPIRIT, AND THE MANIFEST GLORY OF FATHER GOD.

"We decree this house is being filled with the presence of King Jesus. We invite His glory. We declare welcome to the manifest glory of our Father. Fill this house with the cloud of Your presence, with the fire of Your presence. We want and welcome the manifest presence of the Living God. Come. Hover over us. May there be an opening where angels ascend and descend here. Loose them, Lord, to assist the Kingdom of Heaven in this region. Loose them to assist the saints."

WE DECREE THAT WE ARE RECEIVING FRESH POWER FROM AN OPEN HEAVEN.

"Enabling power, come. Creative power, come. Tipping point power, come. Wonder working power, come. Miracle working power, come. Ruling and reigning power, come. Power of God, come into us. We declare it is upon us corporately and individually as believers. We declare God's seed is in us and is activating itself in us right now."

WE DECREE GREAT DELIVERANCE IS BEING RELEASED NOW IN JESUS' NAME.

"We declare deliverance from demon bondage in Jesus' name. Lusts of the flesh, go. Fear, go. Depression, go. Emotional bondage, go. Drugs, alcohol, abuse, go. Sexual addiction, go. Pornography, homosexuality, go. Those spirits are bound. Set us free in Jesus' name. We declare deliverance from poverty, failure, abuse, rejection, grief. Come to this region, Lord, with great power."

WE DECREE ALL GENERATIONAL CURSES ARE BROKEN OFF OF EVERY LIFE IN JESUS' NAME.

"We declare that people from everywhere will come to our churches to be freed from generational curses, and they will experience power that liberates them. We sever those curses. You will not reign over God's people."

WE DECREE THAT OUR CHURCHES ARE BIRTH CENTERS FOR NEW SOULS TO BE BROUGHT TO JESUS CHRIST.

"God's Word will be planted and activated in the lives of thousands upon thousands of people to be born again. Multitudes in the valley of decision will meet the Savior right here at these altars in the name of Jesus. The lost will be found. Prodigals are returning. We call to the prodigals, come back to Father's house in the name of Jesus. We break deception off of you. Let the blindness of soul be removed. Come to yourself, prodigals. Come to yourself and return to your inheritance. Return to your Father's inheritance."

WE DECREE NEW STRATEGIES OF EVANGELISM ARE BEING RELEASED, AND THEY WILL WORK.

"The plowmen, just like Your Word says, are going to overtake the reapers in the name of Jesus."

WE DECREE HOLY SPIRIT POWER IS BEING POURED OUT UPON OUR SONS AND OUR DAUGHTERS.

"It is being poured out on the young, the old, the male, and the female. As Joel prophesied, Holy Spirit power is coming upon our children, teenagers, and young adults. All flesh. The four percent of the coming generation who serve You will now reverse in Jesus' name. We will not settle for that any longer. That generation will rise and serve our God. They will experience a holy visitation and they will prophesy, dream God's dream, see His vision, and they will carry His presence in their generation. Their commitment to Christ the King is going to startle the world, and it's going to be contagious. Awakening, be. Revival, be. Reformation, come and keep on coming. Revival fires, burn through this nation and around the world."

WE DECREE ABUNDANCE, PROSPERITY, AND PLENTY IS NOW BEING RELEASED.

"Covenant blessings, financial success, be released in Jesus' name. Let the devourer be bound in the name of our King Jesus. We decree the windows of Heaven, be open. Blessings come upon and overtake us. Bonuses come upon us and overtake us. Checks in the mail, come. Deals, great deals, come our way. We declare inheritance is finding us in new ways. Stocks and bonds are being blessed and blessed and blessed. Property values, accelerate. We declare in the name of Jesus blessings that have been stolen from the righteous are to return now sevenfold. We declare inheritance, come back and come back

now. What has been stolen, come back and come back now in the name of Jesus. We release blessings to come on us and overtake us."

WE DECREE THE WEALTH OF THE SINNER IS BEING LAID UP FOR THE JUST, AS GOD'S WORD SAYS.

"Prosperity, be. We plant the heavens over us with success and prosperity. We sow abundance and wealth into the heavens and the earth. In Jesus' name we bind lack and we loose abundance. We bind poverty and we loose plenty. We bind neediness and we loose finances. We bind poor living and we loose success. We are ordained to bear much fruit. We decree we are blessed in the city or blessed in the country. We are blessed coming in and we are blessed going out. The Lord commands His blessings upon us as Deuteronomy 28 says. God blesses the works of our hands. He makes us plenteous in goods. He opens His good treasure over us and rains down upon us. It is promised and we say be in Jesus' name."

"Lord, let the church, the ekklesia, the sons and daughters, the born-again ones rise to plant the heavens and the earth with Your words. We will continue to do so, ruling and reigning as You purposed, refusing to allow hell's kingdom to reign over us. We rise today to face and bind principalities, powers, mights, and dominions. We will not say 'baaaa' to them. We will not sheepishly stand for You. We decree Your Kingdom with power, come and reign through Your church in the name of Jesus Christ. We declare it. Amen."

CHAPTER
6

SPEAK LIKE A KING

The Book of Job is the oldest book in the Bible. It was written by Moses, one of the greatest leaders in world history. Moses understood authority. He was trained to be a pharaoh. He was raised in Pharaoh's house, and he understood authority language. He wrote down for us a powerful principle in Job 22:28 that reinforces the dominion mandate that he wrote about in Genesis 1.

> *You will also decree a thing, and it will be established for you; and light will shine on your ways* (Job 22:28 NASB).

> *Thou shalt decree a purpose, and it shall be fulfilled unto thee* (Job 22:28 Rotherham).

> *Now be of use to God; be at peace with Him, and goodness will return to your life. Receive instruction directly from His lips, and make His words a part of you. If you return to the Highest One, you will be restored; if you banish the evil from your tents* (Job 22:21-23 VOICE).

When you approach Him, He will listen; you will make good on your promises to Him. You will pronounce something to be, and He will make it so (Job 22:27-28 VOICE).

I will put together my church, a church so expansive with energy that not even the gates of hell will be able to keep it out. And that's not all. You will have complete and free access to God's kingdom, keys to open any and every door: no more barriers between heaven and earth, earth and heaven. A yes on earth is yes in heaven. A no on earth is no in heaven (Matthew 16:18-19 MSG).

PRAYER

Prayer is decreeing a purpose that God can make so. Quite frankly, I have to remind myself of these principles often because the world seeks to take the church and the people of God another way. The world's government, the media, and of course hell's kingdom hate the message of ekklesia. Very few these days understand that the church is here to rule and reign with Christ *right now*.

Few know and understand this because it's been dispensationalized by many into something that's in the future somewhere, not to be done right now. Very few understand the true purpose of God's sons and daughters or the church that Jesus came to establish. We need to be reminded of some things because we can change and disciple a nation. If we do, our personal lives are going to succeed at much higher levels. Promises that God and Holy Spirit have made to us can be individually or corporately activated. He can make them so, and hell hates that message.

If you do not engage yourself in a conscious way with these principles weekly and even daily, they can drift out of your mind. We've got to have these principles freshly breathed into us, freshly ignited into our spirits, so that they are part of our conscious awareness again. I ponder these things often because I have to apply them rather than allow them to lie dormant in some distant memory. Many in the church allow much of what the Scripture teaches to be in memory only; it's not a conscious activity with them. The principles of faith, authority, and decrees of God's Word are not to be taught so we can *know* them, they are to be taught so we can *do* them. It's time that we do them. Holy Spirit is asking us to do some things.

THE CHURCH'S ASSIGNMENT

We are in a season when clearly we need to *do* the Word of God. The world is divided and crumbling because the church and millions of Christians are not doing their assignment. The world that most of us knew growing up is coming apart at the seams because much of the church has not been doing what God says. We have to be doers of the Word of God. Allow the Holy Spirit to activate this in you.

Job 22:28 again says, *"Thou shalt also decree a thing, and it shall be established unto thee: and the light shall shine upon thy ways."* The Amplified Bible reads:

> You will also decide and decree a thing, and it will be established for you; and the light [of God's favor] will shine upon your ways.

Favor and decrees of faith go hand in hand. Alexander Douay's translation of the Hebrew to English says, *"Thou shalt decree a thing, and it shall come to thee, and light shall shine on thy ways."* That is an excellent translation of the Hebrew language. Decree something and it will come to you. You will pronounce something to be, and God will make it so. That, of course, refers to authority language—the language of kings.

The word for "decree" is the Hebrew word *gazar*, and it means to decide and to purpose. It is also used 11 times in the Hebrew Old Testament meaning to divide, to sever, or to cut off (Strong, H1504). For example, *gazar* is the word used at the Red Sea. It says the Red Sea was cut off. Moses stood in front of the Red Sea and he spoke with authority. He used kingly language and put the dominion mandate into an activated form, a bold command. He raised the rod of authority and he spoke kingly language. He spoke words of ruling authority and he literally said to the sea, "Separate. Open. Divide." Sounds similar to what our King said in Matthew 16:18. You have been given authority to declare things to open or to close. Open things with your decrees.

Job says, "You shall decree a thing and it will be established unto you." *Thing* is a very poor translation. It is the word *omer* in the Hebrew language, meaning to speak, to voice words, to voice promises, or to speak words of commands (Strong, H562). In other words, you shall decree commands and they will be established unto you. You shall decide and give orders of declaration and they will be established to you. God will make them so.

Moses says that what you purpose you must put into words of command, decree them, speak them, and they will be established unto you. Speak like a king in the King's lineage. Speak like you are a joint heir with King Jesus. Speak with the authority Jesus gave us in His name. Come into an alignment with the dominion mandate of God in Genesis from the beginning. In other words, in Jesus' name *gazar*, sever, and cut off hell.

Sever and cut off the attacks of hell with your bold words of authority. Command demons to go. Command them, don't ask. Tell them to go. Command healing to come. Command harvest to come. Command revival to come. Command awakening to come. Speak with authority. Use king language.

QUEEN ESTHER

This principle is presented in the Book of Esther. Esther was a part of the king's household—she was the queen. King Xerxes had signed an evil decree against God's people. A wicked man named Haman was part of his government, and he conspired with others to have an evil law passed and King Xerxes signed it. The law stated that on a certain day anyone could kill any Jew they wanted to kill and confiscate all of their property. The goal was to annihilate God's people, to absolutely remove them from the face of the earth.

Mordecai and Queen Esther were called upon to reverse that evil decree. It's a fascinating story showing the power of delegated authority—legal authority given to someone else and used in the giver's name. It's delegated, but it's real authority.

We need to pay close attention to how words are used. The word *decree* is used ten times throughout the Book of Esther. Nine times the word *decree* is a translation of the Hebrew word *dath*, but Esther's decree is a different word. It is *maamar*, and it is used only one time.

Dath, used nine times, means an edict, a statute, a law, a command, a prescription, or legislation (Strong, H1881). *Maamar* means something spoken with authority. It refers to king's language or a royal edict (Strong, H3982). King's language, authority language, was given to Mordecai and Esther to reverse evil legislation, laws, and government action. Esther 8 tells us that they did use it and they did do it. Authority to decree against and change evil laws was given to them, creating a picture of what Christ did for us through the cross.

As the King's heirs on the earth, we have been restored to use authority language. We have been restored to speak with royal dominion. We have been restored to speak royal edicts for our kingdom. We have received authority in Jesus' name to stop evil prescriptions and laws and to decree God's prescriptions as His kids. We are here to decree God's statutes, laws, ways, and will. We are here to declare God's prescription for our lives, over our assignments, and for our nation. As Christ's joint heirs, we are here to reign in this life using authority language (see Rom. 8:17). *Maamar*—release words of power and authority and make kingly declarations so God can make it so.

We should not be like the man who joined a monastery in which the monks were allowed to speak only two words every seven years. After the first seven years passed, the new initiate met with the abbot who asked him, "Well, what are your two words?"

"Food's bad," replied the man, who then went back to spend another seven-year period before once again meeting with his ecclesiastical superior.

"What are your two words now?" asked the clergyman.

"Bed's hard," responded the man.

Seven years later—twenty-one years after his initial entry into the monastery—the man met with the abbot for the third and final time. "And what are your two words this time?" he was asked.

"I quit."

"Well, I'm not surprised," answered the disgusted cleric. "All you've done since you got here is complain!"

Don't be like that man; don't be known as the person whose only words are negative.

ACCESSING THE KING'S ANOINTING

King David references this authority language quite often in the Psalms. One that is very interesting to me is found in Psalms 26:1. It reads, *"Judge me, O Lord; for I have walked in mine integrity: I have trusted also in the Lord; therefore I shall not slide."* *Not* is an important word to understand. It is the Hebrew word *lo,* which means faint or weary

(Strong, H3808). *Lo* is grammatically used in the Hebrew language as a particle of negation, and it is often seen in the Old Testament.

In other words, it is used to make a positive statement negative. It contradicts a positive statement by injecting negativity into the wording of the sentence. An example would be saying, "I am going to do this, maybe." No, you are either going to do it or you're not. You cannot rule and reign in any kind of ambiguity. Another example is saying, "I'm 100 percent certain, I think." No, you either are or you are not. David said, "I am a king walking before the Lord in integrity and I refuse to be negative or inject negativity into any of my commands. I will not rule negatively."

The King's anointing—which, of course, is Christ's anointing—to rule and reign in this life does not flow through me if I am negative. Negativity will stifle the flow of anointing through you, and God will not be able to do what He wants to do for you. God wants to make you rule and reign, but you can't do that in negativity. David says, "I'm a king and I value the King's anointing on my life, so I will not inject any negativity into my character."

Of course, his character was tested with Absalom and Bathsheba, and he failed in both of those situations, but he did eventually learn from those failures. His confession is clear and powerful: "I will not contradict any sound, upright behavior. I will not compromise my integrity through my actions, and I will not inject any negativity into my words. I am a king, and kings do not make contradictory statements. I am a king, and kings don't double talk. My statements are positive, consistent, and clear. I must make clear rulings."

There can be no confusion or ambiguity. Your words must be decisive. Kings who succeed are not negative. Without question, God's Word states clearly that born-again ones' decrees are very, very powerful if they don't make them negative. There is power to change in our decrees. There is power to reverse legislation in our decrees. There is power to reverse evil laws in our decrees, as long as we don't make them negative.

Authority language was given to Mordecai and Esther to decree a stop to evil laws, to stop an attack against God's people. Kingly language to change a nation was given to them. I see a very strong parallel that pictures the calling of God to His people and to His church right now. In my nation, evil laws are already on the books. Abortion is already a law. Gay marriage is already a law. Even though God says it's an abomination, our legislators have already put it into the law of the land.

Evil prescriptions have been written concerning our culture. Sadly, some are declaring America to be a many-god nation. There is no longer just one God as far our government is concerned. This is not true and contradicts our founding fathers. Clearly, God's people are under attack, and it's amazing how passive we have been. Hamans fill our government, media, and universities, and the bias against God's people is palpable.

Christianity is being defied. Hell is being very, very aggressive, and like Haman it wants to hang the church. It wants to strangle the life out of God's people with evil prescriptions, decrees, lies, and deception. Can we deny that corruption is now rampant in our land? We are lied to with impunity. We have professional liars who now fill public offices in America. Our relevance is scoffed at. Liberal bias against Judeo-Christian values has now filled our education systems and the media.

MEDIA BIAS

Much of the media is now lying to us. Hundreds of examples could be given. Pope John Paul II called the media the modern-day

Areopagus. They pronounce judgment on our Christian values every day. They mock them, they belittle them, and they disdain them. I have personally heard and seen reporters on liberal networks who actually shook their heads and rolled their eyes as they belittled values that I hold dear.

It is crucial that the church hear the challenge and, like Esther, intercede. She prayed and made an appeal. Like Esther and Mordecai, we too must rise up for such a time as this, for we are also facing legislation that brings bondage. Liberty is at stake. Religious bias against abortion is now being defined as "hate speech" and harsh penalties are being suggested. Six thousand years of marriage is now being redefined in our courts. Public prayer is being ridiculed and has been banned from schools and activities. Some have even suggested that we redefine Christianity and modify our beliefs to fit the current culture. Think about that—harsh penalties simply because we believe the Scriptures. Did you ever think you would be punished for believing God's Word? It's now happening.

We are facing corruption in our government. We are facing laws that bring ruin and death, laws that are prejudiced against Almighty God and His people. Yes, word curses abound. They are put into print and spoken into the air every day. A word curse is a statement that belittles, defames, and brings harm and ruin in some way. It's a pronouncement of judgment that causes loss or harm, designed to captivate with thoughts of bondage and fear. We hear them constantly, pounded against God's people by a godless press and, at times, by godless politicians.

FOR SUCH A TIME AS THIS

It is time to reverse the condescending rhetoric and constant judgment. It is time to change evil decrees that cause feelings of despair and end the foreboding. Seventy percent of our nation believes it is going the wrong way. Why not reverse it? It's time for the church to rise up for such a time as this, to do and say what God says, speaking with authority, pronouncing a different prescription. We must rise up in faith and trust our Almighty Great God, ruling in the midst of our enemies. The insanity has got to stop, and it can only be stopped by a real church, not a pretend one.

My prayer is the apostles' prayer in Acts 4:29, *"Lord, behold their threatenings: and grant unto thy servants, that with all boldness they may speak thy word."* Is the church really going to allow the world to tell us what we can preach? God forbid. What if Queen Esther would have refused to act? She would have lost her people—a nation would have gone the wrong way. If we don't act, we could lose our nation.

PROPHETIC WORD

As a word of encouragement I want to share a prophetic word the Lord recently gave me:

> Holy Spirit says to remnant warriors—it is time for the unveiling. The great season has now come and the curtain is being drawn and the world will now see the scintillating Kingdom of King Jesus rising from the ashes of a beguiled world. See it, says the Lord. See its radiant glory. It's intensifying, accelerating, and revealing your King as the supreme commander of Heaven and of earth.
>
> It's time for the reveal of the supernatural into the natural, says the Lord. There will now be seen a spiritual Kingdom that visibly affects the world. It will visibly affect earthly kingdoms. It will visibly affect world leaders. It will visibly affect governments. It will visibly affect the marketplace, the education system, and the media. Like

leaven, the mighty Kingdom of God and His Christ will penetrate the earth as never before.

No more delay, says Heaven. Darkness will now be penetrated and dispelled by glorious light. Deception will be dispelled by glorious truth. Iniquity will be uprooted by glorious power. Demon thrones will be toppled by glorious authority, dominating authority, supreme authority, ruling, and reigning authority. Bondage will be broken by glorious liberty. Curses will now be reversed by glorious blessings. Principalities and powers, mights and dominions will be toppled by the superior forces of My Kingdom, says the Lord of Hosts.

My kingdom is rising, and it will now be revealed in new ways and in new displays. It cannot be stopped. It cannot be hindered. It cannot be compromised. My spiritual kingdom will visibly affect this world. It will rise. It will rule, and it will reign with wisdom and with awesome power. It has been, it is, and it will be increasing upon the earth with jealous aggression and with striking power from Heaven flashing down to your planet, says the Lord. Yes, a Kingdom that has no end and no equal will now be revealed as promised.

The surge of Heaven has now begun. The world has never seen the like; a functioning spiritual Kingdom that's at hand. Yes. You can touch it. Yes, it is among you—a Kingdom that is coming. It keeps coming and coming and coming, and it is coming until an even greater reveal— My coming in the clouds of glory. For you are entering into the season of the mighty King who prevails, a King who will make His stand. His Kingdom is growing and

His Kingdom will prevail. And the prevailing anointing of Jesus will now be seen upon His remnant people.

As in His first ekklesia, so mightily grew the Word and it prevailed, so it will be in your times. Anointing to prevail is now being poured out upon you. You will prevail. The King's Word on your lips will prevail mightily. Speak on the King's behalf. Speak His Word from your lips. Speak as ambassadors in His Kingdom; and as you speak, you will grow. And as you speak, you will prevail.

Increase is increasing. Bounty is abounding; power is compounding. Promises believed for will grow, and they will prevail to fullness before your eyes. Prophetic words will prevail to fullness. My Word will not return void. Supernatural deliverance will now prevail to fullness. Healings and miracles will now prevail to fullness. Dreams and visions will now prevail to fullness. Decrees of your faith will now prevail to fullness. Cries of your heart will prevail to fullness. It is "yes" and it is "amened" by Heaven. My church will prevail, says the Lord. The gates of hell will not prevail. The authority of hell cannot prevail. It is written, and it cannot be reversed. It is the immutable decree of your King, so act in accordant confidence.

Lucifer is not omnipresent, but I am. Lucifer is not omniscient, but I am. Lucifer is not omnipotent, but I am. Lucifer's kingdom is not unshakable, but Mine is. Act in accordant confidence. And I will now lead the greatest move of My Kingdom in all of history. Holy Spirit is now activating My coalition.

I will have My harvest. I will have an allied partnership with Me—remnant champions who will know I am God with them. They will know I have allied Myself and My

Kingdom with them. It will be seen. I am God with them everywhere. I am wisdom and knowledge with them everywhere. I'm the all-powerful one with them everywhere. I'm the prevailing one with them everywhere. They will prevail everywhere; for the coalition forces of My Kingdom have now been called to the battle line. The multiplied strength of My allies joined together for My Kingdom's cause has never been stronger. My angel armies, My remnant warriors, My Holy Spirit, My Father, and all of Heaven have allied with Me and My Kingdom. Fight one of us, you fight us all.

Covenants are now established. Treaties have been signed with My blood. Alignments have initiated assignments, and My allied coalition is strong and enduring. No, hell cannot prevail. My church will prevail. My remnant will prevail; for yes, My Kingdom has been attacked. And yes, My remnant has been pressed in great battle, but know that a mighty Kingdom is allied with you. Know that the King of kings is allied with you. Know that Holy Spirit and His angel armies are allied with you. Know that Almighty God and all of Heaven is allied with you. You will not fight this battle alone. Allies are at hand. Allies are among you. Allies are rushing to the battlefront with you.

My Kingdom, My power, and My anointing to prevail is upon you. You will win against hell's opposing forces. Hell cannot stop you, so arise with My Kingdom and, with great confidence, begin to rule and begin to reign with Me with great boldness, understanding My coalition is behind you. Go and influence earth as My ambassadors. Go and stand for My truth. Go and declare My Word without compromise. Go and make a determined stand for My cause. Go, it is part of My coalition. Rule in the midst of your enemies, says the Lord. Go and in His name prevail.

PRAYER

Decree this prayer:

Lord, let Your surge begin on the earth. Let a functioning Kingdom aligned with You begin to move through this world. Come to us in greater manifestations of Your glory. Make Your stand with us as You promised.

As kings in His lineage given authority, we declare there will now come a reversal of arteries that are all clogged up. Release thousands and thousands of angels to go into every county, every courthouse, every capital in every nation and rip off the Band-Aids. No more temporary fixes. No more covering it up. Cut it out. Do deep surgery on this nation, O God. Release them to help push back darkness so that light can shine. Do what is necessary to remove infection and poison that goes into the muscle of this nation. Shake this nation to its core. Shake it, Lord, to where there is no more covering up. Heal it. Do whatever it takes to heal it. No more Band-Aids.

Let Your church awaken. Awaken Your people by the millions to make a stand right now to raise their voice and decree their authority, their faith, and their confidence in You. Cause a historic shift that will be written about in history—the time when You established this nation back to its covenant roots.

In the name of our King Jesus, release the angels of Heaven under Holy Spirit anointing and leadership to destroy tactics of Haman in the media or government. Turn it back on them, what is meant for destruction. Hang them in their own vices.

Hang them from gallows they meant for Your people. Cut off hell's attack. We forbid it in Jesus' name. We close the door to powers of darkness over Washington, D.C. We close the door to the powers of the demon princes of hell in the name of Jesus. We say that our angel princes that are mightier than you will go in and begin to remove the infection.

We declare a reversal of the prescription of hell for this nation. The prescription of Haman for this nation. Expose the lies. Expose the liars. Expose the corruption. Expose the deceit.

We declare America will return to You. We will return to our first love. Your people will return to their first love. People, Lord, all around this world will return to their first love. Those who have drifted from You—shake them up, do whatever it requires. Quit allowing them to put a Band-Aid on the corruption of their heart. Expose attitudes and character. Expose lack of integrity.

We declare the greatest days of resurrection power and healing are now being released. We declare a restoration of great hope is being infused in the church of Jesus Christ and into the people of God.

We declare Your Kingdom is coming and coming and coming. Come with your angel armies and assist Your people in releasing revival in America and throughout the world. We rise to bind demon thrones, principalities, powers, demons of darkness, and spiritual wickedness in high places. You will not rule us. You are forbidden from ruling us. We will not permit it. Greater is He who is in us than he who is in the world. Come down from your iniquitous thrones. Demon princes, come down from your strongholds. Angel armies, attack them! Let the ruling Kingdom of God go forth to conquer. We choose to rule and reign.

We will not be intimidated by any fear. We will not be intimidated by anyone. We will not be intimidated by Hamans in the media, the government, or anywhere else. We answer only to You, God. Strengthen us to be courageous and make our stand. Release Your Kingdom to reorder this nation back to its covenant roots in Jesus' name.

CHAPTER

7

COME HERE

Decrees create. They can create ideas in your heart. They create things that are not seen with the natural eye. They can create changes in conditions and in the atmosphere physically, spiritually, emotionally, materially, governmentally, politically, vocationally, and provisionally. Decrees are a creative force and they release a creative force that will bless us abundantly.

In Isaiah 42:9 God says, *"New things do I declare: before they spring forth I tell you of them."* Notice that He says, "I declare them before they spring forth. I pronounce them before they ever are." Smith and Goodspeed's translation reads, *"New things I foretell—before they spring into being, I will announce them to you."* So God says, "I announce them. I declare without negation first so that they can be seen."

The New Jerusalem Bible reads, *"Fresh things I now reveal; before they appear I tell you of them."* The Knox translation says, *"I tell you now what is still to be; you shall hear it before it ever comes to light."* God says, "If it is to be, if I have purposed it to be, I will speak it first before it ever comes to life." First comes a decree—a declared word that He will not change or negate. The Living Bible reads, *"I will prophesy again. I will tell you the future before it happens."* That's what prophecy is—foretelling something before it happens. Anyone can prophesy after something happens. God says, "I explain with My words what is to be before it ever is, and then it springs forth and materializes. It doesn't materialize until I speak it. It doesn't materialize until there's a decree." That's what Hebrews 11:1 is about—faith decreed becomes substantive. Faith-filled words materialize if you don't negate them.

The word *before* in Isaiah 42:9 is the Hebrew word *tehrem*. It is a very important word for believers and the church to understand because it means "suspended in time" or "not yet occurred" (Strong, H2962). So God says, "While its existence is suspended in time, while it has not yet occurred, I decree it."

The two words *spring forth* are from one Hebrew word—*tsamach*. It is an agricultural word that means to sprout, to bud, and to grow to fullness (Strong, H6779). It indicates a process that will come to fullness, to maturity. It first sprouts, then buds, and finally it grows to fullness when it's decreed or planted. It will not come to fullness until it is decreed. The word *tell* is the Hebrew word *shama*, meaning to sound a message, to announce something, to proclaim, or to voice (Strong, H8085). In order to create, you have to voice it. Before it occurs, announce it. While it is suspended in time, while it has not occurred yet, you have to announce it. It will never produce what it is if you don't plant it and decree it.

This principle is clearly shown in Romans 4. In this chapter, the apostle Paul was talking about words of faith that create, produce promises, and change things. These words cause us to overcome and live very successful lives. They cause promises to materialize. If you want promises to materialize in your life, you must understand these principles.

C.J.'S STORY

For many years, I lived in an apartment complex. I was the sole provider for myself and my three children. I had many neighbors moving in and out, some not so nice, and my desire to buy a house grew stronger and stronger. Most years were spent dealing with the fear of not being able to manage the upkeep of owning a home. I did get my finances in order to assure my credit standing was good, but I did nothing else to move forward with this dream. I did begin to rehearse over and over in my heart and say out loud, "The Lord is my Shepherd, I shall not want." One day I decided I had conquered my fear and I put a bid in on a condo, thinking I didn't want the yard to take care of. But to my surprise the bid was rejected, and I felt too insecure to pursue it. More years went by, and I reminded Him of His word promise to give me the desires of my heart, however He wanted to accomplish it, and I lived in expectancy.

I recited almost daily, "I AM Alpha and Omega, the beginning and the end, saith the Lord, which is and which was and which is to come, the Almighty." I would say, "Lord, no one else can say that and it be true. The Lord is my Shepherd; You take care of me. You will give me the desires of my heart. I'm reminding You of Your Word, Lord." These were words I lived by. I was under the covering of my pastor, and I stood on the Word.

Years later, circumstances made it highly unfavorable for me to remain in the apartment. I began bringing boxes home from my job, and my coworkers asked me if I was moving. I said, "Yes." They said, "Where to?" and my response was "I don't know." The truth is, I began packing my belongings, and at the time I had nowhere to go. I just knew I was not staying where I was. I was totally dependent on the Word of God and I believed His Word.

To shorten the story, I found a house, closed on it, and my grown children moved me into it within 30 days. All of my children have stated that it feels like we have always lived there, even though at this time they are all adults and in their own homes. I never fail to thank the Lord for His faithfulness. God has given me the desires of my heart, provided for me in every step along the way, including a new roof, better job, healing—all because I make my confessions based on His Word. I declare and pray His Word, and He is my Shepherd, I shall not want. —C.J.

In Genesis 22:18, God told a man named Abraham—Abram at the time—that he was going to be the heir of the world and the father of nations. Notice that this was before Abram ever had a son, and God decreed this to Abram when it was impossible for him. Abram was 99 years old and Sarah was 89 years old, well past the age to bear children. But God isn't bound to any limitations. He wasn't bothered by what Sarah and Abram looked like or their age. It didn't matter.

While having a child was suspended in time and before it occurred (*tehrem*), God prophesied it. While it looked impossible, God announced it. He declared it. He spoke authority words of faith. He created what was impossible for man with His words. You must decree words of faith first in order to create promises that are impossible where man is concerned. You must declare what seems impossible in the natural realm to see it materialized. Then it can spring forth, sprout, bud, and grow to fullness.

The promise will remain impossible, suspended in time, until it's decreed. The moment it's decreed, it becomes possible. When the promise is decreed, it is conceived—it goes past mere knowledge and becomes substance that is planted and can grow.

Romans 4:17 says, *"(As it is written, I have made thee the father of many nations,) before him whom he believed, even God, who quickeneth the dead, and calleth those things which be not as though they were."* That is one of the most loaded statements in all of Scripture. Understanding it is of paramount importance to moving in faith and creating things that don't exist with your words. God's declaration was, "I have made you the father of many nations." It is done. You are a father. There is no ambiguity in that statement. There is no "maybe" and nothing negative injected into it. God went so far as to say, "Change your name from Abram to Abraham because Abraham means *father of a multitude*." God decreed what He expected to see, even though it looked impossible to man.

The principle is very clear—we are to decree what we expect to see, using authority language. We have to live like who we truly are—the sons and daughters of God. Much of the church is passive where their faith is concerned, waiting to see something before they decree something. But, you cannot see if you don't decree. It's just not possible.

The principle is clear in the lives of Old Testament saints as well as the New Testament saints. It is also clear in the life of our King Jesus. If you want to see promises materialize, then you have to decree them without negation. You must declare them *done* in His name.

I often hear someone who is believing for a promise say, "But I don't see any evidence of this." Exactly! That is the point! You don't see any evidence because it is suspended in time. It doesn't exist yet. Quit looking at that. You cannot see evidence until you plant a decree. But people say, "Well, if I say that, I am lying." No—you are creating it, not lying. Don't negate it, create it.

In the beginning, God didn't see trees and then tell us about trees. There were no trees. While they were suspended in time, He said *"be"* and they sprang forth. True faith calls it *done* in Jesus' name, and then the promises can sprout, bud, and grow to fullness. What seems impossible becomes possible, ready to be watered by our faith and brought to fullness.

Romans 4:17 reads, *"God...calleth those things which be not as though they were."* The New English Translation reads, *"God who makes the dead alive and summons the things that do not yet exist as though they already do."* He summons or calls to them. That is the best translation. That is what the Greek text describes—decrees summon something to come to you. Authority language summons what does not exist yet to come to you. It speaks of it as being done. The Living Bible reads, *"God...speaks of future events with as much certainty as though they were already past."* Then it says, God *"calleth those things that be not as though they were."* *Calleth* is the Greek word *kaleo* and it means to say out loud, to bid, to call something near you, and to summon (Strong, G2564).

The phrase *those things* is translated from one Greek word in the original text—*ousa,* meaning to be and being (Strong, G5607). But it primarily means to come. So when you put the two together, *kaleo ousa* would mean "come here" or "come to me." Say aloud, *"Come here. Come to me. Come here now."*

In verse 17, *not* is the Greek word *me* (pronounced like "may"), and it means no existence, nothing, and to deny (Strong, G3361). Faith says to things that have no existence, "Come here. Come here now." Faith summons them. It says to promises that demons are trying to deny, "Come here." It commands, "Demons, you go, take your barriers down, and I summon the promise to come to me." Apostle Paul is teaching you to see promises come to you and materialize. Two times he declares, "Here's how you do it. You have to say come here, come here."

We must use kingly language toward nonexistent things or things that must be changed. In Jesus' name, we are to boldly decree—to things that are suspended in time, to promises that have not been fulfilled yet, to prophecy that has not occurred yet—"Come here and manifest to me."

Read this awesome testimony from our youth leaders at the church I pastor.

ROBERT AND CHELSEA'S STORY

We knew from the moment we were married that we did not want to wait a long time to begin our family. Pretty early on, Chelsea became pregnant and we were so excited. Not long into the pregnancy she began to have some symptoms, and then we lost the baby. After I found out that Chelsea had a confirmed miscarriage, I did my best to comfort her. As a man, the husband, the situation is different, I believe. I was just as confused and hurt as Chelsea was, but it took place inside her body so, of course, she was going through a whole range of feelings and emotions, as well.

Later that night, I felt something so strong inside of me telling me to go pray. This was more than just taking a walk and praying. This feeling was, "Go get alone with Me and pray!" I told Chelsea and off I went. I went to the church gymnasium where we meet with the youth. I didn't turn on any music. I turned on one light and it was just me and God. I sat in silence for about an hour. I didn't know what to pray. I didn't know whether to ask for understanding or decree healing. I didn't know. But the more I sat in silence, the more Pastor Tim's sermon "No More Delay" filled my thoughts. It began to overwhelm my thoughts first, and then it overwhelmed my heart. I stood up and began to decree that very thing. "No more delay." I said it over and over and over again. I then began to call our son by name. *River.* "Come to me, River. Come to me. Come to me, son. Come here, River." Over and over again. God was present. It was more than just me praying to God. I was speaking to our situation. I was speaking life into our hearts' desire, and that was to have a son. When I left, I knew it was as good as done and I would get to meet little River very soon.

Just a short time later, Chelsea was pregnant again and now we not only have River, who is ten months old, but we are expecting our second son, Gunner, in just a few months. We are beyond thankful and blessed for all He has done. —Robert and Chelsea Sabo

I have been given hundreds of prophetic words over the years, and I use this principle constantly, declaring, "You come to me and you materialize. You will come here and you will materialize. You are going to take on substance and you are going to grow to fullness. You cannot stay away from me; you have to come here. Come here, come here. Come to me!"

As believers, we need to begin to declare, "Come here and come here now." To promises that hell's kingdom may be denying you, you've got to start saying with bold authority, "Come here. Come to me, healing. Come to me, finances. Come to me, new job. Come to me. Manifest. Take on substance. Sprout, bud, and grow. I am not going to make this command negative any longer. I'm not cancelling. In Jesus' name, you come here."

You can easily see the commanding authority language that we are supposed to be walking in. What do you do when you feel your rights and privileges are being denied to you? You are to arise and speak in this manner, "In Jesus' name, come here and come here right now." Decree the promise is yours. Proclaim that the promise is yours and don't negate it. The Scriptures plainly teach that decrees come first. You have to decree before it's ever conceived. Proclaim the promise and then it materializes. It doesn't materialize until it's decreed and not negated.

The apostolic teaching is clear from Romans 4:17, and the Greek text rendering is very authoritative. The Greek says, "Bid come here to things still to be or to rights that are being denied you. Do so in this manner, do it this way—in Jesus' name, come here and come here right now. Materialize for me." Wow. That is a powerful faith decree!

JOSHUA'S STORY

When our son, Joshua, was four years old, our family doctor, Dr. Les Kresge (an elder in our church at the time), detected a heart murmur during a routine office visit. He sent us from his office directly to Children's Hospital in Cincinnati because he knew what he was hearing was not a typical heart murmur that many children have and outgrow. After a series of tests the surgeon told us that Joshua would need a coarctation of the aorta. He had a narrow place in his main aorta, so they would need to do open heart surgery to clip out the narrow part and reattach the normal sized parts. He said Josh would need to grow for a couple of years before they could do this, in order for his aorta to be large enough for the operation not to have to be repeated later in life. During this growing time he would need to be watched closely because in essence this was a life threatening condition; it could cause either a stroke or sudden death. It was devastating news. Carol and I took him home and then I went out the lake, my favorite place to pray. I knew I needed to worship, pray, and decree over our son. During this prayer time a song was birthed in my spirit from Revelation 15:3-4. The song went like this:

"Great and marvelous are Thy works, O God,
Just and righteous are Thy ways.
O Thou King of Saints, who shall not fear Thee
We lift our voice in praise to Your name."

We made a decision to not live in fear for the following two years. We worshiped and we decreed His Word over Joshua. I sang it over and over and then taught it to our church and we all sang it. We had people all over the nation joining us in prayer, speaking healing words over Josh. When he was six years old the doctors determined it was time for the surgery. They opened our son's chest and repaired the aorta. The surgery was successful, but Joshua could not wake up. He was attached to the heart/lung machine for two days while we waited for him to open his eyes. I went into the chapel located in the hospital and made decrees over him. After 48 hours he finally woke up! That was a monumental day for our family. After seven days we were able to take our son home and he is perfectly healed today. Indeed, great and marvelous are Your works, God!

It may take us a while to get the revelation of our promise. We know it took Abraham, the father our faith, a while to get the revelation, but he did get it. Abraham had to hold fast to that promise, as Hebrews 10:23 instructs us: *"Let us hold fast the confession of our hope without wavering, for He who promised is faithful"* (NKJV). The Greek for "hold fast" is important to understand. It is the word *katecho*

(Strong, G2722). *Kat* is the word meaning down—down in your spirit, your guts, or your middle (Strong, G2596). *Echo* is the Greek origin of the English word *echo*, meaning to hear over and over and over again (Strong, G2192). You don't shout a word and the echo starts repeating other words. No, it's the same word echoed time after time. In other words, Abraham echoed the promise of God over and over and over again. He held it fast and he literally said to a nonexistent son who had been suspended in time, "Come here. Come here and manifest, Isaac. You come here and you materialize for me." He said it until verse 21 says he became fully persuaded.

> *And being not weak in faith, he considered not his own body now dead, when he was about an hundred years old, neither yet the deadness of Sarah's womb: he staggered not at the promise of God through unbelief; but was strong in faith, giving glory to God; and being fully persuaded that, what he had promised, he was able also to perform* (Romans 4:19-21).

It says he *"considered not"* the condition of his body or Sarah's body. The word for "considered" is *katanoeo,* and it simply means to contemplate or to observe something in the mind (Strong, G2657). He shifted his thinking away from conditions that his mind presented to him. He *"staggered not"* at the promise through unbelief. The word for "staggered" is the Greek word *diakrino,* meaning to separate, to withdraw, to oppose, to hesitate, to contend with, or to differ (Strong, G1252). He didn't differ with the promise of God in his words. He didn't withdraw the promise of God by speaking different words. He didn't oppose what God said with his thoughts. *Katanoeo* comes from the root *nous* (Strong, G3539, 3563). These definitions reminded me of the English word noose, something that strangles the life out of you. Don't let negative words hang you. They will stifle creative abilities that you rightfully have as an heir. Abraham just kept saying, "Come here, come here, come here."

Before Isaac was conceived and born, Abraham began decreeing his faith. The Hebrew commentators tell us he actually did this out loud. Can you picture this old man coming out of his tent every day for 25 years? The promise has been nonexistent all this time, and yet he shouts loudly, "Come here, Isaac. Materialize. You come here and you come here now. Come to me." His faith summoned and beckoned Isaac.

Romans 4:21 says he became "*fully persuaded*" that what God had promised He was able to perform. "Fully persuaded" is the Greek phrase *plerophoreo*, meaning to convince or win over with words (Strong, G4135). God won Abraham over with His words. We could say that He spoke winning words to Abraham. Interestingly, it has an implied reciprocity in the Greek language. In other words, when Abraham spoke winning words to God, planting them in the heavens, God spoke winning words back to him. Abraham declared, "I win," and God echoed it from Heaven, "Yes, you win."

Thankfully, God never speaks to us with words of condemnation. He doesn't call us losers. He doesn't say to us, "You can't make it. You are now going to fail. You're a failure. You're going to be overcome." No, it's *plerophoreo*. When you believe what God says and you decree it, God says you win. You are a winner. You're an overcomer. You will now succeed.

When you put faith in the promise of God, God begins to speak winning words to you. Winning words begin to rise up in your spirit against the negative words of your mind. The winning words of God in your spirit begin to overcome, and you begin to win and succeed. God speaks winning words to you. He says, "You are a winner. You cannot lose. You are a champion. You are a conqueror. You're victorious.

You're triumphant. You're an overcomer. You are going to make it. You are going to get this done. You are an achiever." We are to echo back to Him in agreement, "I am a winner. I can't lose. I'm a champion. I'm an overcomer. I'm victorious. I'm triumphant. I'm healed. I'm an overcomer. I'm going to make it. I can do it. I will achieve this goal. I will get this done. Miracles are materializing for me."

Many today have promises suspended in time that haven't occurred yet, but we are to say to them, "Come here," and not negate it. If the people of God would dare to do what He said and begin to declare "Come here," we would see great creative promises begin to spring up all over the place. But so often negative words come to our minds and go out of our mouths, surround our necks, and strangle the life out of our faith. Don't do it. We are to refuse to look at the conditions. If you look at the conditions, you are going to get very discouraged. You could look at the condition of our nation and get very discouraged. Instead, look at God. Observe what He says and all the promises He has made to us.

These are the greatest days in church history. When are we going to declare that? Ponder His ability to perform His promise. Rise in authority language and bid promises *come here, come here, come here*. If you want to see promises sprout, bud, and grow to fullness, get hold of the principles of faith (not just in a knowing way but in a doing way). It's amazing to me how many people know what faith is and yet don't do it. Choose today to activate your faith and say, "I am going to do it and I am going to see the promises of God materialize in my life. I am declaring *come here, come here, come here*."

8

DON'T GET NAILED

How forcible are right words!
—JOB 6:25

Authority words are very powerful. The right words are forcible and release destiny when declared. They release purpose and they help shape your future. It's one of the most powerful lessons that you can learn from the Scriptures. Planted properly, right words will empower your life and release more and more of your potential. Your potential will remain latent if you do not release the right words. Right words will prod you toward excellence, fulfillment, and success.

God made humans in such a way that words affect us spiritually, physically, and emotionally. Words affect the mind, the will, and the emotions. They affect the actions that we take in life, sometimes in dramatic ways. Our entire being responds to the force that is in words.

Words can affect you for the good or for the bad. They can inspire your life to move forward, or they could deflate your life so that you go nowhere. The right words release power, pushing you toward your purpose that God helps you discover and live out.

The Scriptures teach very clearly and powerfully that God wants His sons and daughters living out their lives on the earth with great purpose and meaning. He desires for His heirs to live with a sense of destiny, peace, and joy, knowing that goals set before them can be reached. His laws of life and the dominion mandate that He has given from Genesis 1 will work for us. It will work for any born-again one if it is applied. No one is exempt. Word seeds will grow and produce for us. Authority language will work for us, and our lives will experience the results.

DESTINY AND POTENTIAL

As far as God is concerned, your future is very bright. Your life is to be lived out in a very good, peaceful, gracious way. Your destiny is good. There are no disasters planned for you. His plans for you are good and hope-filled. Your potential is absolutely awesome.

From the very beginning in Genesis 1, God has designed it so that the potential He has placed inside of all of us is activated by the words of faith we speak and by actions of obedience in line with what God says. There is so much potential in the world today. Every single one of you is loaded with potential. Potent power is in you to be something you've never been before or do something you've never done before.

Word seed decrees will help create your future. Your words are seeds that produce after their kind. Destiny words, along with words of success and purpose, can grow to fullness when believed and acted upon. They prod you to produce. They germinate, grow, and reproduce themselves.

DAVE'S STORY

One morning in August of 2012, I walked into work as I normally do. On the way to my office I looked down the hall and saw the president of the company, my boss, going to his office as well. He did not speak a word to me and barely looked at me. I knew at that moment something was wrong. I actually felt in my heart that I would be losing my job that day. I actually said to myself, today is the day. This stems from a staff meeting the previous week where we were told that the finances were not good and that some changes were on the way.

I went home that day for lunch and told my wife, Linda, that I felt it would be my last day at work. (She was home due to the fact that she lost her job of 14 years just three months earlier.) She could not believe that I would lose my job after 24 years of employment, especially after I had worked my way up through the company holding various positions, earning a degree in mechanical engineering during my time of employment and ultimately becoming the quality manager of the company. Sadly, I returned home early from work that day, unemployed. I found out later that I was not the only person to lose their job.

As my wife and I stood in the kitchen that day, devastated and heartbroken, all we could do was say that God has to have something better for us. The hard part was believing that God had something better for us. At times this was a very difficult thing to experience because neither of us had ever been unemployed, much less at the same time.

We faced financial obligations that would not be covered by the small unemployment checks that we received. In order to pay off some debt and to have money to live on, we had to dissolve our retirement funds as well as the severance pay that Linda received from her employer. I still remember our discussion about paying tithes on this money as well as our unemployment checks. Being unemployed was not going to be an excuse to disobey God. We were going to pay tithes, even on the retirement funds!

Early on in Linda's 18 months of unemployment, she decided to go back to school. As she was talking with a counselor at the school, they had told her about a program in her county that may assist with her tuition. This was a true Godsend; not only did they pay for Linda's tuition, books, and travel mileage, they also paid for my Lean Six Sigma Black Belt certification, which in their eyes would make me a more marketable candidate.

I was blessed with a job, after being unemployed for six months, where I made more money and received better benefits than I had from my previous employer of 24 years. I stayed there for three years and three months before accepting another position elsewhere. About two months before I left this employer I was offered a quality manager position at another company, which I accepted. This was an agonizing time for me for I had never quit a job and really wondered if I was doing the right thing, so I declined the job one week before I was to start.

Less than a month went by and I really felt that I needed to get out of where I had been for the past three years. I ultimately accepted a position and left, making more money and receiving better benefits yet again. One week after I left the company that I had been with for the past three years, they lost their biggest customer and multiple people lost their jobs.

During our time of unemployment, Linda and I prayed, decreed, and believed for the rich jobs to come forth. We paid our tithes and believed God for our future. Although this was a very difficult thing to go through with all of the feelings of rejection and worthlessness that satan wants you to believe about yourself, I believe that we have place-holders in life so God can place us where He wants us.

—Dave Collinsworth

IDLE WORDS

Jesus makes a powerful and sobering statement concerning how important it is to speak life to yourself:

For out of the abundance of the heart the mouth speaks. A good man out of the good treasure of his heart brings forth good things, and an evil man out of the evil treasure brings forth evil things. But I say to you that for every idle word men may speak, they will give account of it in the day of judgment. For by your words you will be justified, and by your words you will be condemned (Matthew 12:34-37 NKJV).

On the day of judgment men will have to give account for every idle (inoperative, nonworking) word they speak (Matthew 12:36 AMPC).

Every one of these careless words is going to come back to haunt you. There will be a time of Reckoning. Words are powerful; take them seriously (Matthew 12:36 MSG).

As born-again ones, we know that when we stand before God we will give an account for certain actions. I don't think many understand that we will also give an account for the words we speak. This leads us to a word that we need to understand—*idle*. Here, it is the Greek word *argos*—a particle of negation. Remember that King David said that he would not rule negatively or inject negativity into any of his decrees. To inject negativity into a decree, you put the word *not* before it. *Idle* or *argos* is a particle of negation in the Greek language, and it means inactive, unemployed, useless, barren, nonworking, and unprofitable (Strong, G692). It would mean *not* active, *not* working, *not* profitable. Jesus said we will answer for useless, negative, or idle words.

Idle words cause promises to be nonworking and inactive in us. Negative words are unprofitable. Notice that Jesus said if there are negative thoughts in the heart, they will proceed from your mouth. Negative thoughts are going to come out of your mouth and cause promises to become barren. *Argos* does not produce life that is abundant; it produces un-life, not-life, or un-fulfillment. It would produce un-success, empty desires. Negative words bring about a forfeiture of benefits.

Jesus also said, *"For by your words you will be justified, and by your words you will be condemned."* *Justified* is the Greek word *dikaioo*, and it means to set forth as righteous because of receiving Christ's payment for sins (Strong, G1344). The born-again ones are made to be righteous because of the shed blood of Jesus and Calvary. We are made to be righteous and are due certain rights because we are now heirs—heirs of God and joint heirs with Christ.

RIGHTS AS HEIRS

There are certain privileges that are due to us. You have privileges that are due to you as an heir that are not due to anyone else, not even angels. Angels aren't sons or daughters; they are created beings that can be godly, but they are not heirs. *Dikaioo* also means to cause, to become, to make, or to free. In other words, your words make for your quality of life. They life you or they un-life you. They free the promises, life, and benefits due to you as an heir. Your words shape you. If you speak the right words, you will live life well.

The root of *dikaioo* is *dike*, which is a legal promise of rights that are self-evident (Strong, G1349). In other words, these rights are clear and common sense. It's also the word for justice. We must speak words of life and faith as Christian citizens and heirs if we want the rights we deserve because of our right-standing with Christ Jesus. Words that agree with God's Word free promises to produce what they are.

If we instead speak negative words of unbelief that disagree with what God says, contrary to our rights as heirs, Jesus said, "By your words you are condemned." The word for "condemned" is the Greek word *katadikazo*, and it is more New Testament legal language. It is the Greek word meaning judgment and to pronounce a sentence (Strong, G2613).

Amazingly, Jesus says, "Your words can sentence you." You are sentenced to live what you say. What you speak can bind up your life or loose your life. It can life you or un-life you. You can sentence your life to barrenness, with very few kingdom promises coming your way. So—are you sentencing yourself to live in lack and poverty? To live depressed, unjoyful? To live sick or diseased, unhealthy? To live in hopelessness, not wellbeing? To live in fear, not security? To live in defeat, not victory? Are you sentencing yourself to this through your own words? These are sobering questions.

This New Testament principle says we are destined to live the life we speak from our mouths. Someone may ask, "I thought God controls our destiny. Isn't that what David said in the Psalms? Isn't that what Jeremiah said?" Not exactly. God has planned a great destiny and purpose for you, but that doesn't mean you will automatically live it. It only manifests to the point you agree with it, to the degree you plant proper seeds and live in alignment with what God says.

As born-again ones we are destined to live in divine health—spirit, soul, and body. But that doesn't mean that we always do. Our words must agree with God's destiny in order for it to germinate and grow to fullness. We must contend for it in prayer with authority language, resisting opposition in the natural realm and the spiritual realm. We must contend for it with declarations of faith in what God says, no matter what our circumstances look like. We must speak kingly language without negation in order to live in our destiny because we have an adversary who tries to steal our benefits.

Third John 2 says, *"I wish above all things that thou mayest prosper and be in health, even as thy soul prospereth."* It is certainly God's purpose that born-again ones prosper, but you're only going to prosper to the level that you agree with God's destined prosperity and obey Him—bring the tithe, bring offerings, and decree your faith. You're a born-again one and prosperity is due to you, but it's going to be barren unless you do what He says.

SPEAK RIGHT WORDS

Jesus was saying, "There is a time of reckoning. Words are powerful. Take them seriously." Every promise in the Bible is conditional upon whether or not we believe it and decree it. Our mouths must say what God says. Our text said in Job 6:25, *"How forcible are right words!"* The word for "forcible" is the Hebrew word *marats,* and it can be used negatively or positively. It's a picture word in the Hebrew language that means "to press" (Strong, H4834).

In those days, the king would wear a very special ring upon his hand—a signet ring. The seal of the king's kingdom was engraved on the face of the ring. It was a governing ring. When important documents were brought to the king, he would stamp the document with it, leaving behind the seal of his kingdom. He would press his seal on it.

I wear a signet ring; in the last fifteen years, I haven't preached without wearing this particular ring. On the face of this ring there is engraved in Hebrew letters the name *God Almighty* because that is the Kingdom I work for. I represent the Kingdom of God. Although we use a notary seal today, over the years when important documents have been given to me to sign, I like to discreetly tap the document with my ring as a seal stating, "Done, in the name of our Kingdom." Also, throughout human history coins have been minted by stamping a print into little bits of heated metal. The Hebrew idea is that words do the same thing. They leave impressions and they seal things.

God's words are always right words. When we meditate upon God's Word, when we roll it around and around in our minds until we are renewed by what He said, it begins to penetrate our hearts and our spirits. God's Word leaves an impression. It leaves its seal in us. Then out of our hearts, Jesus said, our mouths speaks and agree with the impression God's Word has left there.

WORDS OF LIFE

The right words will press our problems to conform to the promises that are in our hearts. The right words will be forcible and change situations, activating the promises of God and stamping the seal of God's promise on the problem. The idea is to press the problems to conform to God's Word by declaring your faith. Right words carry the weight of the Kingdom of Almighty God behind them.

In Ecclesiastes 12:11, the aging King Solomon wrote, *"The words of the wise are as goads."* A goad was a long stick that was sharpened to a point like a spear, and they would use this goad to make their oxen or cattle move. Today, they use electric cattle prods, but back then they just sharpened a stick. Solomon said that the words of the wise are like that. Their words keep them moving toward their purpose, goals, and success. Their words keep them from standing still and becoming stagnant. Their words keep producing for them. Their words prod them forward and onward, steadily plowing through to victory.

Solomon also says the words of the wise are *"as nails fastened by the masters of assemblies."* We would call them master carpenters or builders today. A master carpenter knows where to nail something together. He makes his nails work for him. Solomon said that's what a wise man does with his words—he nails down the promise of God with his words. He makes words work for him. Just like nails are used to hold boards in place, words are used to hold promises in place. Nail down God's answer for your problems with the words of your mouth. Decrees are your nails. They nail God's promise in place. Nail your adversary, your opposition, and the situation. Nail it with God's Word, with the promise of the Living God.

WRONG WORDS

This can also work in a negative way. Many of God's kids are influenced by pessimistic decrees. They talk doubt and unbelief. They talk about how rough they have it, how bad things are for them, their insecurities and fears, how no-good their life is, and how poor they are. They confess Murphy's Law—whatever can go wrong probably will. What happens? The devil nails them. Millions of God's kids today are getting nailed.

Benefits due to them are barren, and one of the reasons is the words they speak. It's interesting that the word *marats* (forcible) can be used in a negative way as well as a positive way. When used negatively it means to irritate. Wrong words irritate you, your life, and your destiny. They irritate your wellbeing, your peace, your joy.

Back in high school, I loved to play sports. I played basketball, football, baseball, and ran track. I played sports and studied on the sidelines a bit because I wanted to pass, not fail. I remember a common statement we used when playing football. If someone was carrying a ball and another guy tackled him extra hard we would say, "He got nailed." My junior year I broke my ankle on a kickoff return. Why? Because I got nailed. Don't get nailed with your own words. Say what God says. Speak words of faith. Speak words of life to yourself and they will germinate and grow.

Wise King Solomon also wrote in Proverbs 6:2, *"Thou art snared with the words of thy mouth, thou art taken with the words of thy mouth."* The two words *snared* and *taken* have similar Hebrew meanings— to be caught in a trap and captured (Strong, H3369, H3920). They literally mean to become a prisoner of war. Wrong words can snare you, causing you to become a prisoner of war, bound up, ineffective, unable to move as you want. Wrong words allow demon traps to snare you. Your words can either work for you or against you; they'll either nail down the promise of God for your life, or you're the one who will get nailed.

A wise man uses his words like a master carpenter and makes his words work for him. His words become like well-driven nails that build a strong and secure house. He uses his words to build life into himself and into his family. He uses his words to create a blessed world to live in. Your words are indeed forcible.

ANOTHER JOSHUA STORY

When our son, Joshua, was about a year old, he came down with bacterial meningitis. He had been sick, and we thought he had the flu. Although he hadn't been feeling well for a few days we went to church that Sunday morning with Carol keeping him in the office while service began.

We had a guest speaker that morning, so when our family doctor arrived for service I asked him to step into the office and take a look at Josh. He did, and then he said we needed to get Josh to the emergency room right away and he would accompany us there. Needless to say fear tried to rush in. Before we left the service we stepped in with Josh and asked for everyone to pray for him. We then rushed out to the hospital. Once we were there, they began to run numerous tests, and then a spinal tap was done. They had their diagnosis, and it was meningitis. The next step was to determine what kind. Blood tests were run to the point they were drawing from his tiny little heels to get more blood. Carol had to go up three floors to get away from his screams, and I did my best to comfort him. They found it was bacterial, and treatment began. Everyone tried to warn us of possible side effects, including hearing loss or even deafness—but God! Everyone we knew was praying and decreeing words of life and health over him. After nine days he was released and doing totally fine, no side effects whatsoever! This was indeed miraculous, as our doctor told us later that Josh was within hours of dying when he sent us to the hospital. During this time, another song was birthed in me:

> *"O Lord, our God, how great and how wonderful*
> *You are the Great I AM, reigning today.*
> *O Lord, our God, the Master of everything*
> *We lift our voice and sing*
> *We let our praises ring*
> *We call You God and King, Savior and Lord."*

Today Joshua is a healthy young man with perfect hearing, totally healed and restored. The Word works!

SPEAK GOD'S WORDS

God's Word itself is possibly the most valuable source of word seed decrees that will life you and your faith. We need to learn to decree the Scriptures in such a way that they are personalized into our lives. It's a very simple thing that I have practiced for about thirty years now. I spend an hour or more doing this at least a couple times a month. It has blessed my life and helped me through some very difficult times.

I often read these passages and then personalize them. For example, most people know Psalm 23, "The Lord is my Shepherd." But when you put that in decree form it starts to transform your life and feed you in a different way. When I put it in the decree form after reading it, it sounds something like this:

King Jesus is my Shepherd and I don't want for anything. I want for nothing, and I will never want for anything because my King Jesus is my Shepherd. He makes me to lie down in places of great resources that will only feed my life. That will happen to me this day. He leads me beside the still waters. He will never lead me into troubling places. He leads me to restful places and He restores my soul. No matter what comes to deplete me, my King will be there to restore and life me afresh and anew. He will lead me in great paths today—paths of righteousness. Right ways will be before me, and I will be led down the right path; even if I walk through the valley of death, I fear no evil. I will not fear evil. I don't have to fear any kind of evil because He is always with me. I fear no evil. His rod, His staff, they are always there to comfort me. Even if I come into the presence of my enemies, I will have nothing to fear because He will spread a banquet for me. He will resource me anyway, no matter what situation I find myself in. He anoints me with fresh oil. My cup is going to run over. The anointing of the

Kingdom of God is overflowing and running through my life. Goodness is following me everywhere I go. Mercy is following me everywhere I go. Favor is following me everywhere I go, and it will be that way all the days of my life. I will dwell in the house of the Lord forever because I am a part of His family. I am a son/daughter of God. I have a right to be in His house. His presence is where I live. Because I live in His presence only good will come my way.

That is a decree based upon the Word of God, and it is so easy to do. Just follow along and declare it, and when you do the Word will reset you for what is ahead. Your words will line up with God's Word, and when something happens you will find yourself decreeing what God says. Another example is Psalm 91:

I dwell in the secret place where the presence of God is. I dwell there. I live there. I come where God's presence is, and I abide under the shadow of the Almighty. I come under the wings of Almighty God. I am close enough that the shadow of God is upon me today. I am in His presence. And I say of the Lord— You're my refuge. You're my strength. You're my Defender. I will only trust You. You are the one I trust. You are my source. You are going to deliver me from any of the snares that the adversary is putting in my way. You're going to reveal them, and then by Your power you're going to scatter and shatter them by the breaker anointing that is on Your life. You're going to deliver me from pestilence. You cover me with Your feathers. Under Your wings I take refuge. Your truth, Your Word, is my shield and buckler. I will not be afraid of things that come out of darkness and jump my way. I'm not going to be afraid of arrows that are shot toward my back because You're my rear guard. A thousand could fall around me, but it's not coming at me. No evil will befall me. No plague will come nigh me. He gives His angels charge concerning me. He keeps me in all of my ways. I will be kept in all of my ways. Angels are circling all around me to deliver me. I'm not going to trip over anything. I'm not going to dash my foot on a stone and trip around. I'm not tripping over anything. I will walk steady and secure because He has set His love upon me; He will deliver me. And with long life He will satisfy me, which means I'll probably still be preaching when I'm ninety.

Those are life decrees right out of Scripture. You set yourself with those and they life you. Another one, Romans 8:35:

Nothing can separate me from the love of God. Nothing can. Nothing can do that. Nothing can separate me from His love. Tribulation can't. Persecution can't. Famine can't. Peril can't. A sword can't. I am more than a conqueror in Christ Jesus. I'm more than a conqueror because of Him who loved me and gave Himself for me. I'm an overcomer. I'm a conqueror. I am persuaded, I am absolutely persuaded; death can't take it away. Nothing can. Angels, principalities, powers, things present, things to come—doesn't make any difference. No height, no depth, nor any creature shall be able to separate me from the love of Christ Jesus. Nothing can.

This will life you. You can do this with any Scripture. With stories it's more complicated, but you can take the point of the story and say *that's mine,* as in Isaiah 53:

Surely my King bore all my griefs and He carried every one of my sorrows. I don't carry them. I don't have to and I'm not going to. He carries my grief. He carries the sorrow meant for me. He was wounded for my transgressions. He was bruised for my iniquities. The chastisement for my peace was put upon Him, and by the stripes on His back I am healed. I am. He took them for me. I am.

Personalize the Word. Make decrees of faith and watch how it infuses your life to move in a different way. Say what God says. It will life you.

CHAPTER
9

THE FORCE OF WORDS

My brethren, let not many of you become teachers,
knowing that we shall receive a stricter judgment. For we
all stumble in many things. If anyone does not stumble
in word, he is a perfect man, able also to bridle the
whole body. Indeed, we put bits in horses' mouths that
they may obey us, and we turn their whole body. Look
also at ships: although they are so large and are driven
by fierce winds, they are turned by a very small rudder
wherever the pilot desires. Even so the tongue is a little
member and boasts great things. See how great a forest
a little fire kindles! And the tongue is a fire, a world of
iniquity. The tongue is so set among our members that
it defiles the whole body, and sets on fire the course
of nature; and it is set on fire by hell. For every kind
of beast and bird, of reptile and creature of the sea, is
tamed and has been tamed by mankind. But no man
can tame the tongue. It is an unruly evil, full of deadly
poison. With it we bless our God and Father, and with
it we curse men, who have been made in the similitude

of God. Out of the same mouth proceed blessing and
cursing. My brethren, these things ought not to be so.
—JAMES 3:1-10 NKJV

James says, *"Out of the same mouth proceed blessing and cursing."* Your words will either bless you or they will curse you. Obviously, we ought to be using our mouths to bless our lives. Don't allow any word curses to come into your life from yourself or anyone else. Over the years, people have word cursed me a few times. I change it by saying, "I cancel that in Jesus' name because I can only be blessed." Don't allow word curses in your life.

In 1984, my wife Carol and I went to Seoul, South Korea for a church growth conference. Dr. Cho pastored the world's largest church there for years. It's an amazing place. At that time he had over 600,000 members. They were having seven services on Sundays with 50,000 people in each service. It was phenomenal to see.

After the Sunday services, we started the pastors' and leaders' conference, and Dr. Cho decided he would take all of the leaders out to Prayer Mountain. They had actually purchased an entire mountain and named it Fasting and Prayer Mountain. There is a huge chapel there that holds about 5,000 people. We got on buses and traveled to Prayer Mountain. Before we started a three-hour prayer session, Dr. Cho spoke to us on a fascinating topic. He had recently met with a neurosurgeon who was explaining to him new breakthroughs they had discovered concerning the mind and the power of words. The neurosurgeon told him that they had discovered that the speech center of the brain affects all the other parts of the body. It even helps control the nervous system of an individual.

Words affect you. The doctor said that human beings can manipulate their entire bodies by simply speaking and declaring words. He gave some examples and said that if someone keeps saying, "I'm weak and insignificant," every cell in the body receives the message, "It's time to be weak." The entire nervous system and all of the cells begin to prepare themselves to become weak because that is what was communicated from central control and that's what happens. They begin to adjust their attitude for weakness and weakness actually begins to flow throughout the body. If someone says, "I'm a nobody. I just don't have any abilities," their entire being receives the message that they are a nobody and have no ability. So they don't act properly; they don't respond to situations like they could because they think they're a nobody. When things happen in their life they say, "I can't handle this. I'm a nobody." Their entire being begins to submit to the words they have declared and live out wrong words.

When I came back from Korea, I decided to do a study on this because I was fascinated by it. I learned some amazing facts about authority language. Research shows that if you speak negative words or you have negative thoughts, the brain releases a chemical that begins to penetrate your entire being. It is called a catabolic hormone. A catabolic hormone is a chemical that breaks down body tissue or body cells. Negative thoughts or negative words actually break your body down. If you continue to speak them you can actually make yourself sick. You can change your mood. If you sing the blues, you release that to your entire being. If you want to meditate and think upon and confess and talk about how bad you have it, you can actually bring yourself into a place of depression.

On the other hand, if you have positive thoughts and you speak positive words, the brain signals the release of anabolic hormones, which help you heal. When you speak right words, positive words, faith words, healing is released to the entire body. Anabolic hormones flow through the cells of your being, making you feel better and energized.

Proverbs 4:22 says it this way—God's words *"are life to those who find them, and health to all their flesh"* (NKJV). Thinking on and decreeing what God says allows healing to flow through our entire body. Right words are very important. Proverbs 17:22 says, *"A merry heart does good, like medicine"* (NKJV). A good, cheerful disposition is health to the body. A mind that is set to God's Word allows healing to begin to accelerate as health flows to the whole body.

I also discovered that healing, anabolic hormones are released during two other occasions—when we laugh and when we sing. That is why singing your praises to God is so important—it *lifes* you. Ever come into church and you're just not feeling that great? Maybe you feel down or sick? And as you start to sing praises to God, before long you start to feel better. You start feeling energized. You begin to sing and your mood changes because something is being released. God made you this way. That's why it's so important that you sing songs of praise. Sing! It energizes you and releases power for healing throughout your entire body. Of course, you have to sing the right things. You cannot sing, "I was drunk the day my mom got out of prison,"[1] and expect to feel better! You have to sing the right words.

Remember, songs are words, and words affect your life. Dr. Mark Chironna writes:

> The trajectory of your life and your destiny is insepa-
> rable from the words that begin in your heart and then
> flow from your lips. Be very aware of the words you uti-
> lize to describe your emotional states. The way you label
> and describe your emotions has a profound effect on the
> outcome you actually experience and the way others

experience both you and your influence. Transform your words, and everything is transformed.[2]

Years ago, I was invited to watch open heart surgery at Kettering Hospital. The story of this is now a song that has gone around the world called, "Tell Your Heart to Beat Again."[3] There was a man in our church who was on the open heart surgery team, and he asked if I wanted to go and watch open heart surgery. Of course, I said yes. I don't know how he got me in, but he did. In open heart surgery, the surgeon stands on one side of the patient and everybody else is on the other side. No one stands over the head of the patient, so that's where they put me. I was looking straight down into the chest. I was as close as the surgeon was as I watched the surgery.

The bypass surgery is very simple—they find a place in the heart that is blocked and they put a hole on one side of the block and one on the other. Then they get a piece of vein and just go around the block—it's a bypass. It's like plumbing. I was fascinated as I watched everything. One older man had a triple bypass, and the surgery went smoothly with no complications. I watched another man's heart bypass and it also went very well. Then I watched a quadruple bypass of an elderly lady, and it was something I will never forget. The surgeons and nurses were just talking during the first two surgeries. While they were working, I was thinking, "Hey, wait a minute. Pay attention!" But on the third bypass everything got really tense. You could tell something was wrong—she wasn't responding. They were trying to get her off the heart-lung machine, they needed her heart to start beating and they weren't succeeding. The surgeon began to massage the heart; then he put saline bags around it and tried to warm the heart, but he couldn't get it to begin beating. He then did something I will never forget. He leaned over and called her by name and said that she needed to tell her heart to beat. As soon as he said it, boom! It started beating. I was fascinated to say the least. I couldn't wait to get out of there and ask him some questions.

When we got out of the surgery room, I asked if he could tell the difference between someone who goes into surgery with a great positive attitude and those who do not. He said, "Oh, absolutely!" He gave me a couple of examples. There was one man they were pushing out for surgery who looked at his wife and said, "Well, I'll probably never see you again," and he said goodbye. The doctor bumped him from the schedule and sent someone to tell him that he must not say that because they lose people on the table that way. It is very important to go in with the right attitude. He also told me about when the Cincinnati Reds were in the World Series and there was an older lady scheduled for surgery who loved the Reds. She told him, "I want you to go in and fix it and take me back to the room because it's an afternoon game. I want my lunch delivered, and I'm going to watch that game. So whatever you do, go in and fix it." And he said, "So help me, she did." She woke up and said, "Get me to the room." She sat up in bed and ate lunch and watched the Reds. So he said, "Yes, I can tell the difference between those with a right disposition and those with a wrong one." Right words matter. Disposition that is set according to the Word of God matters. Right words are forcible.

A woman in our church, Debbi Jeffery, recently had an experience that illustrates this point so well. Shortly before a Sunday morning service she told my wife, Carol, that she was scheduled for a heart procedure in two weeks and she was nervous about it, even dreading it. That morning I spoke on this topic and used the illustration, "Tell your heart to beat again," in the context of planting the heavens with your words. At the end of the message she came up for prayer, and as I got to her in line Carol whispered to me what Debbi had told her prior to the service. Of course, I had no idea of their conversation when I was preaching, but every word I spoke to her that morning ministered to her. We laid hands on her and prayed and decreed and said several times, "So be it." This is the rest of the story in her words.

DEBBI'S STORY

I was diagnosed on June 20, 2016 as having bradycardia, a condition where the heart beats at a slow rate, less than 60 beats per minute. On June 22, I was fitted with a heart monitor for two weeks. After the two weeks the cardiologist read the results from the monitor and ordered another test called a tilt-table test, which is used to trigger the symptoms when you have a low heart rate and feel faint in order to see what needs to be done to improve. I failed this test and was referred to a cardiologist heart rhythm specialist.

At this visit, I was advised that I had numerous events on the monitor of my heart dropping into the 40s and 50s. Most of them lasted from five to nine seconds. I was told I needed to have an ablation procedure as soon as possible on the right side of the heart. This procedure is done by scarring the tissue in the heart to correct the rhythm. I was scheduled for September 28, 2016.

On September 18, I got up to go to church and an episode hit me. I was very dizzy, lightheaded, and felt like I was going to faint. I laid back down in bed and the Lord spoke to me that I needed to go to church. So I got up, got ready, and went to church. Praise and worship was wonderful and you could feel God's presence. Pastor Tim got up to speak and in part of his message he talked about the healing of the heart and how words heal. It hit me hard and I knew that's why I needed to be there on that Sunday. At the end of the message he gave an altar call for anyone who needed prayer for anything. I went forward and he and Pastor Carol prayed for me. Carol told him about the upcoming procedure; he had no idea. He prayed for me and I felt the healing touch of God. At the end of the prayer he looked at me and said, "So be it."

On September 28, the day of the ablation, I got up and felt very scared and again dreading what was in store for me at 2:30 P.M. All morning, I doubted my healing and even questioned if I would come through this. I knew I needed to get into the Word, and Psalms 100:5 was the verse I landed on. I just needed to believe I was healed. After reading a few more verses, Pastor Tim's "so be it" kept popping into my head. My sister had also requested prayer for me on Facebook that day and hundreds of people were praying for me.

We arrived at the hospital and the doctor was running behind. In the pre-op room it was already an hour past the scheduled time. At that point exactly I turned to my husband, Al, and decreed, "I am healed!" I wanted to leave but knew I had to go through with it and it would be a witness to the staff and doctor. A nurse told me it was going to be uncomfortable, even painful because I was only having a local anesthetic. As the doctor began to work on me, I was wide awake and stayed that way for two and a half hours with no pain whatsoever. All during that time, the doctor was trying to recreate my heart problem in order to do the ablation. He finally told me that he could not create the low heart rate and the closest he could come only lasted one second, not the five to nine seconds that occurred on my heart monitor. He was completely dumbfounded because he had nothing to repair. He told my husband this happens very, very rarely. While still on the operating table I took the opportunity to tell the doctor and the seven nurses with him that I was healed through prayer, stating, "God is my Healer." Word decrees work.

—Debbi Jeffery

James, the brother of Jesus and the leader of the Jerusalem church, wrote about the importance of our words in A.D. 49: *"For we all stumble in many things. If anyone does not stumble in word, he is a perfect man, able also to bridle the whole body. Indeed, we put bits in horses' mouths that they may obey us, and we turn their whole body"* (James 3:2-3 NKJV). The emphasis here is on the whole body. The tongue, the speech, and the words of our mouth are compared to a horse's bit and bridle.

If you have ever ridden a horse, you know that one of the ways that you control that horse is through the bit and the bridle. If you pull the rein to the left, the horse goes to the left. If you pull to the right, then it's going to go to the right. If you pull back a bit, it comes to a stop. The words of our mouth are compared to the bit and bridle—we are controlled by them. We're pulled one way or the other by the words that we speak. Our words have the ability to stop us or give us free rein to move. They control the whole body. Every part of our being, James says, is controlled by the tongue and the words of our mouth. Then he says in James 3:4, *"Look also at ships: although they are so large and are driven by fierce winds, they are turned by a very small rudder wherever the pilot desires"* (NKJV). Our words here are compared to the rudder on the bottom of a ship. The little rudder of a great big ocean liner will turn that boat any way the helmsman desires. Our words are the same way. We are turned in the direction that we desire by the words of our mouth.

The Bible says God wants to give us the desires of our heart, but it's our responsibility to steer our lives toward that desire with our words. So many times we say things with our mouths that are not our desire. Someone may say, "Well, I'm so weak and insignificant, but my desire is to be great for God." Well, your desire alone will never get you there. You could desire something for the rest of your life and never pursue it and achieve it. Your words are the rudder that will steer you to your desires. Your words are the bit and bridle that will guide you toward the desires of your heart. If you want to do great things for God, you are going to have to talk like it. You have to use authority language. Your central communication center is going to have to tell your entire being, "You can do this. You can do great things. You can be successful. You can do all things through Christ who strengthens you." Activate your entire being to pursue your desire with right words. Say about yourself what God says about you. It starts to steer you toward your desires.

This principle is why you must declare the visions that you have for your individual life or business and most certainly the vision God gives you concerning your future. The prophet Habakkuk was told, "Write the vision in bold clear letters so it can be read on the run. For the vision of the future will speak. It will not lie; wait for it—it's on the way" (see Hab. 2:2-3). In other words, believe it's coming to you. Declare that it's coming to you. Like Abraham, the father of faith, declare, "Come here, vision. Come to me. Manifest. Come here. Come here now. Come here, vision. Manifest to me. Be here now."

In 1979, I began my first month of pastoring The Oasis. I began to realize I needed to declare vision for the future of our church. We had 11 people at the time; actually we had 22 but when they made me the pastor 11 of them left. I thinned them out. I'll never forget on a Wednesday night one lady stood up and said, "Not being personal, but we don't want you. We want somebody dynamic." I thought, "How are you going to get somebody dynamic for 22 people?" So they were stuck with me.

On my second or third sermon, I decided to declare vision. I got up and I said we were going to buy a lot of land and build a building that would hold two or three thousand people, and we were going to be a New Testament church for the region (at that time I didn't understand apostolates) because Joel's revival was coming and we were going to affect thousands and thousands of people. I can say that today, nearly four decades later, and now that it has happened we can all say, "Hallelujah!" But when you have eleven people, that doesn't have a lot of punch. But I just kept saying it. I printed it. I declared it. I read it. And I started to run with it.

Like King Solomon said, those words began to goad me. They prodded me. When things didn't look good and I was tempted to just forget it, I felt this sharp pain in my backside goading me. There were times when it didn't look so good. After two years we had up to 100 people, and I was thinking I would never affect thousands of people. What is this about? Just forget it! But these words, the decreed vision, was like a spear in my behind. "You said this is what you're going to do. You said this is where you're going. You even said God said it. You can't stop, and if you're tempted to stop there's a spear." Every day I felt it. I was tempted to stop and I felt the words rise up, "Move it! Go! You have to act!"

Though opposition came and the temptation was to back off, thinking *it can't be done* or *we don't have any money*, I felt this sharpened stick saying, "You have to move. You keep going this way." This is why you have to declare vision—once it's declared it's hard to not do it. If you don't declare it and nobody heard anything about it, it's easy to give up on it. But once it's declared it begins to goad you. It begins to prod you. I couldn't lay around doing nothing because declared vision was jabbing me—"Get up, pursue the vision."

I'm still declaring vision today. I still declare it almost everywhere I go. The greatest days in church history are not in our past; they are in our present and in our future. I still declare awakening and reformation. I've declared it and declared it for ten years. At my age, people wonder when I'm going to slow down. I can't slow down; there's a spear behind me. When I start to slow down it says, "You have to get going. You said we are going to change this nation. You can't settle down. You have to move it." I'm tired—*move it*. I don't want to—*move it*. Get going. It becomes a prod—you declare it and it begins to energize your entire being. *Move it.*

James 3:6 also says that the tongue can defile or corrupt the whole body. The Amplified Bible says that wrong words *contaminate* the whole body. If you speak fear, your whole body is going to be contaminated with fear. If you speak unbelief, your whole being is going to be contaminated with unbelief. Your whole being is filled with the words of your mouth producing after their kind. Whatever it is will be produced. It's a law in perpetuity. It works. It always does. Our words, our tongue, our speech will either bless us or curse us.

King Solomon adds emphasis in Proverbs 18:21, saying, *"Death and life are in the power of the tongue."* The potential for life and death are both present. Your words will either bless you or curse you. They will either produce life or they will produce death. They are under the power of the tongue. "Power" is the Hebrew word *yad*. It means "in the hand of" or "under the direction of" (Strong, H3027). It's like a musical director who stands in front of an orchestra and tells trombones, flutes, violins, and each section when to come in. He sets the tempo and determines how loud it's to be or how soft. He is the director, and he's in control. The lead pastor of the church in Jerusalem wrote, "Death and life are under the direction of the tongue." The tongue determines which it's going to be—blessing or cursing. It's under the power of the tongue.

Amazingly, this apostle says life is directed by the tongue, by your words. Proverbs 12:6 says, *"The mouth of the upright shall deliver them."*

Why is that? Because the mouth of an upright man speaks right words and right words are forcible. Right words are words that agree with God's Word implanted into our heart, and those words decreed in Jesus' name bring deliverance. Proverbs 10:11 says, *"The mouth of a righteous man is a well of life."* Proverbs 12:18 says, *"The tongue of the wise is health."* Proverbs 13:3 says, *"He who guards his mouth preserves his life"* (NKJV). Right words preserve life, destiny, prosperity, health, and vision. Proverbs 16:24 says, *"Pleasant words are like a honeycomb, sweetness to the soul and health to the bones"* (NKJV). The welfare of your entire being depends on the words of your mouth. Your words life you. Your life, health, wellbeing, and destiny are determined by your words.

One of the greatest examples of how words affect purpose and release potential in our individual lives comes to us from one of the world's greatest minds—the great inventor Thomas Edison. Edison struggled as a child in school. His teacher even called him "addled" to his face—an old-fashioned way of saying he was mentally handicapped. Edison told his mother about it, and she was furious. She went to the school with him and argued with the headmaster, but he wouldn't change his verdict on her son. Edison's mother promptly withdrew him from school and decided to educate him herself. She believed one hundred percent that not only was her son not "addled," he was brilliant. She rejected that label and gave him a new one to live by, and Thomas Edison became the greatest inventor of his time and reshaped the world as we know it.

Words are powerful. Words release potential. Words open up more destiny to you. Words establish vision. Release anabolic hormones in your life. Do it out loud with courage. Decree these words:

> *I am everything God says I am. I can do everything God says I can do. I will speak with my mouth what God says about me.*

I am healthy. I am righteous. I'm at peace. I am wise. I am prosperous. I'm successful. I'm an heir of God and a joint heir with Christ. I'm a conqueror. I'm a winner. I'm an overcomer. Holy Spirit lives in me. His power is at work in me. Therefore, I live my life in victory. Amen. So be it.

NOTES

1. David Allan Coe, "You Never Even Called Me by My Name," by Steve Goodman and John Prine, Columbia, 1975, vinyl recording.

2. Dr. Mark Chironna's Facebook page, accessed February 14, 2017, https://www.facebook.com/drmarkchironna/posts/10150663945349946.

3. Danny Gokey, "Tell Your Heart to Beat Again," by Bernie Herms, Randy Phillips, Matthew West, BMG Records, 2014, CD.

CHAPTER
10

BUILDING BLOCKS

And Jesus answering saith unto them, Have faith in God. For verily I say unto you, That whosoever shall say unto this mountain, Be thou removed, and be thou cast into the sea; and shall not doubt in his heart, but shall believe that those things which he saith shall come to pass; he shall have whatsoever he saith. Therefore I say unto you, What things soever ye desire, when ye pray, believe that ye receive them, and ye shall have them.
—MARK 11:22-24

Then Jesus said to the disciples, "Have faith in God. I tell you the truth, you can say to this mountain, 'May you be lifted up and thrown into the sea,' and it will happen. But you must really believe it will happen and have no doubt in your heart. I tell you, you can pray for anything, and if you believe that you've received it, it will be yours.
—MARK 11:22-24 NLT

Jesus replied, "Have faith in God [constantly]. I assure you and most solemnly say to you, whoever says to this

165

*mountain, 'Be lifted up and thrown into the sea!' and
does not doubt in his heart [in God's unlimited power],
but believes that what he says is going to take place, it
will be done for him [in accordance with God's will].*
—MARK 11:22-23 AMP

That's an incredible statement—what you decree will be done for you.
That blows my mind if I really allow myself to focus on it. It is possible
to live in this promise. Jesus is defining authority language here. It is
not a principle only for the five-fold ministry; it's not a principle for the
socially elite or for government leaders; it's a nonexclusive statement
made concerning each and every Christian. If you are born again, this
statement is about you. It is also a timeless word because it is an eternal word—it will always be true. So this verse is for you right now. Do
not dispensationalize this. You are one of the "whosoevers" who can
command mountains to be moved. You may not feel like it, you may
not think so, you may not believe this, you may never put this promise
into practice, but it is a word for all heirs and it is potential Christian
living for everyone who believes it.

In 1986, we were beginning construction on our church building,
and a mountain of opposition arose. It was fierce. We were meeting in
our old facility and doing two services in the morning on Sundays and
one in the evening. We were completely out of room. We decided it was
time to build. We had gotten a loan to fund it, but things started to go
wrong. The building contractor missed his bid by about $800,000 and
the heating and air conditioning guy missed his bid by about $75,000.
He put a lien against us, and it froze our bank accounts. Because I
made a public statement that we had to raise cash to pay the bills or we
would default on the loan, the heating and air conditioning guy sued

us for two million dollars. Additionally, a construction worker fell on the job site and was killed. His wife sued us for 18 million dollars. At this point, we had 20 million dollars in lawsuits, we were about a million dollars in the hole, and everything was shutting down. There were piles of construction supplies everywhere. We were six years old at the time; we had no money and couldn't get the money we should have had access to. We were all locked up. I don't know if that qualifies as a mountain in your view, but it did to me.

I remember not knowing what in the world to do, so I began to pray. I walked the sanctuary of our church at the time and prayed. I did that most of the night and the next day too. I was just going to pray all night, "God, You have to come through. I don't know what to do. I see no way out of this. I felt like You gave us a word and You spoke to us and allowed us to grow. But everything's locked up and there's nothing I can do." That second night I was praying, and about two in the morning I walked to the job site. I stood where our current platform is now. At that time it was a huge pile of sand. I climbed up to the top of the pile and sat there in the dark by myself. I just prayed, "God, do something. Show me something to do."

Earlier that day I had been studying Philippians 1:28, *"In nothing terrified by your adversaries: which is to them an evident token of perdition, but to you of salvation, and that of God."* The word *nothing* there is the Greek number zero (Strong, G3367). "In zero terrified." *Perdition* means loss or ruin, but it also means loss or ruin that is forever irreversible (Strong, G684). What Calvary has done for us is forever irreversible. Satan can't come and reverse what Jesus did at Calvary. Deliverance and salvation were provided and are forever irreversible. Our victory is irreversible. I remember jumping up onto the pile of sand and screaming as loud as I could into the night, "Satan, our victory is irreversible. Calvary makes it irreversible. We are going to beat you. We are going to win."

I wish I could say that the mountain moved instantly, but it didn't. Most mountains don't. Most of the time it seems like it's a process. The mountain-moving process began. The judge threw all of the lawsuits out, unlocked our accounts, and gave us favor to begin again. We finished this and have preached the Gospel all around the world many, many times. That mountain was not possible in the natural realm, but our victory was irreversible. Spiritually this is possible. God can do it and He has done it.

> *Truly, I am saying to you, Whoever says to this mountain, Be lifted up and be thrown into the sea, and does not doubt in his heart but believes that that which he says comes to pass, it shall be his* (Mark 11:22-23 Wuest).

> *"Have faith in God," replied Jesus to them. "I tell you that if anyone should say to this hill, 'Get up and throw yourself into the sea', and without any doubt in his heart believe that what he says will happen, then it will happen!"* (Mark 11:22-23 PHILLIPS)

I don't see any bail-outs in that statement whatsoever. I don't read any "yes, maybes" in the statement. Whatever you believe and decree will happen. That's astounding. I'm glad Jesus made this statement. If He hadn't said it, we might doubt it. A part of the Godhead said it, not some pastor somewhere. Jesus said it, so God definitely meant for you to know this. This was not a slip of the tongue or a divine oops. He wants you to rule and reign with Him (see Rom. 5:17). He wants you releasing authority language, you exercising your dominion as an heir, and understanding that in His name you can summon to you what does not exist yet. You can also command things to go from you that do exist. You are authorized to use authority language. *Mountain, go there and go there now. Hindrance, get away from me. Come here, go there.* We have authority to summon or to send away. We can send away from us what hinders our benefits from getting to us. It may take some time, it may take some spiritual warfare, it may not always be easy, but we cannot say that it is impossible.

We have looked primarily at summoning blessings to us, but sometimes there are things that have to be dispatched or sent away in the name of Jesus. We have to send some things packing. Spirit of poverty, go from me. Spirit of heaviness, go from me. Depression and hopelessness, go from me. Fear, cancer, disease, demon activity of every kind, oppressive adversity that attempts to strangle our purpose and destiny, our future, hopes and dreams, we are to exercise authority and dispatch it from us in the name of Jesus. It is subject to the word of faith in our heart being declared. Clearly, God wants us to act on our authority. It's a part of the Dominion Mandate that those in authority have power to command to come or command to go.

Jesus said, "Whoever shall say to the mountain." The word for "say" there is the Greek word *epo*, meaning to speak with authority, to command, and it pictures a general or a king who stands before troops and gives a command or an order to them (Strong, G2036). It means to tell and to order. Jesus said that those in authority, His heirs, can command things to come or to go. They can command, tell, or give orders to mountains or to obstructions that come to hinder their lives.

Mountain is the Greek word *oros*, and it means to rise, to lift up above the plain, and to rear up (Strong, G3735). A mountain is an obstacle that rises, rears up, and blocks our pathway. It could be a sickness, disease, financial trouble, a job loss—anything. We have authority to command it to go, change, or make a correction in accordance with the Word of God—to turn and actually become good for us. Any mountain that rises up, you have authority to decree "Go" to it in Jesus' name, and you have authority to command it to begin to align with the Word of God. "Conform to the promise of God in my life. Come to me now and manifest."

Mark 11:23 also says, *"Whosoever shall say unto this mountain, Be thou removed, and be thou cast into the sea; and shall not doubt in his heart, but shall believe that those things which he saith shall come to pass; he shall have whatsoever he saith."* Saith is two different Greek words in this statement. The *"things which he saith"* is the Greek word *lego*, and it means to speak by linking together the inner thoughts and the inner feelings of the heart and the mind (Strong, G3004). *Lego* means expressing the heart and the mind with words.

Perhaps as a child you played with some toys called Legos. We have some Legos at our house, and I play with them. Our younger grandchildren—Lily, Jude, Jaidin, and Joelle—love to play with Legos. They like to dump them all out at the same time because you never know which piece you are going to need. Legos are building blocks, and you can connect the pieces together and build whatever you are thinking—a truck, a car, a soldier, a fort, or a castle. You build whatever you want. Authority language is the same. Use your words to build with. Build what your heart desires by expressing it with your words. Lay foundations and frame what you want with your words.

Jesus says, "Like I framed the worlds in the beginning, you do that." That's what Hebrews 11:3 says: *"The worlds were framed by the word of God."* Describe what you want. Build your heart's desire by framing it with your words. Jesus describes your words as building blocks. You are going to build something with them—good or bad. The contents of your heart that you speak will be laid forth, framed, and built. Part of the imagery here involves construction, which is natural for Jesus because He was a carpenter. He used those terms often. Why are mountains moved in the first place? Bulldozers move mountains to build a road, a shopping center, or a home. Jesus and the Godhead are saying, "Stand in your authority and order mountains to be removed; then build what's in your heart by decreeing and framing it with your words."

Words are pictures of the visions in your heart, snapshots of the dreams inside of you. They explain your goals and build the concepts that are inside you. They are the blueprints that build your future. Build it with authority language. Systematically build a good life around you with your words. Jesus gave us a divine principle that He Himself practiced in His life and in the very beginning. You can order mountains to move and build a good life around you with your words.

"He shall have whatsoever he saith" is the word *epo* again—to command like a general, to *"say unto this mountain"* (Strong, G2036). "You shall have what you speak with authority. You shall have what you command in My name," He says. "You shall have what you order in My name if you don't negate it and doubt in your heart; it's going to come to pass," He says. It will sprout, bud, and grow to fullness.

The King says, "Arise and command hindrances that rise in your way to go, and then build a good life around you with your words." Connect your sentences together in a systematic faith language, framing the desires of your heart that agree with God's promised blessings for your life and what He says you can have. Declare your benefit rights as an heir. Frame them. Build them. Don't tear down with your words—build with them. Systematically connect the sentences of your mouth to the faith that is in your heart. Speak your faith. Release words that will work for you and create victory in your life. Command problems to go and build answers by decreeing what God says. Obviously, the heart and the mouth are connected. God made it that way. Your mouth gives voice to the heart, spirit, or soul. Your words describe what's in your heart.

> *A good man out of the good treasure of his heart brings forth good; and an evil man out of the evil treasure of his heart brings forth evil. For out of the abundance of the heart his mouth speaks* (Luke 6:45 NKJV).

In other words, if your heart is filled with doubt and unbelief it will systematically connect to negative sentences from your mouth. If doubt is in your heart, negation will proceed from your mouth. But if your heart is filled with God's Word and words of faith, then that is what you will speak. Your mouth mirrors what's inside of you. If you have more of the world's information inside of you than God's Word and His ways, then it's going to show in the words you speak, write, or think. It's going to show on your Facebook page. Most of the time you can listen to someone's conversation and tell how they are doing. You can listen to how someone talks and tell if they are believing God or not because their mouth will either mirror unbelief or faith. There is a connection. If something is in the heart that shouldn't be there, it is going to be reflected in the mouth. If bitterness or unforgiveness is in the heart, it is going to be mirrored in the mouth. If discontentment or fear is in your heart, it's going to be reflected in your words. If you listen you are going to hear it. Out of what's abundantly in your heart the mouth speaks.

Proverbs 18:21 says, *"Death and life are in the power of the tongue."* Both are possibilities. We can build life or we can tear it down. Sadly, many Christians tear their lives down. Proverbs 10:11 says, *"The mouth of a righteous man is a well of life."* A well has water that can quench thirst and preserve life. Draw up life and quench thirst. Draw up refreshing. Draw up deep resources with your words. Pull good life forth with words of faith from your heart.

Proverbs 15:4 says, *"A wholesome tongue is a tree of life."* Wholesome is the Hebrew word *marpe*, meaning cure, medicine, remedy, health, deliverance, or to mend (Strong, H4832). Curative words are a tree of life, and living trees produce fruit. If the tree is alive, it's going to produce its fruit. Produce *marpe* with your tongue. Produce it with your words. In other words, "Come here, cure. Come to me. Come here now. Health, come. Body, mind, and soul, mend now. Speak remedies.

Medicine, come. Healing, come. Healing process, accelerate." Speak curative words that will become fruitful medicine producing life.

God has given great grace in the area of healing. It can come to us in all kinds of ways—through God's Word, laying on of hands, medicine, herbs, rest, diet, doctors, or surgery. Choose one that is in your heart that you believe, then declare it to accelerate and manifest. The believers, the heirs, ought to be decreeing health.

Proverbs 12:6 says, *"The mouth of the upright shall deliver them."* *Deliver* is the Hebrew word *natsal,* and it means to free oneself, to recover, and to rescue (Strong, H5337). Your words can build recovery into your life. Recovery can sprout, bud, and grow to fullness. Maybe you have a lot of losses—you can frame recovery to come and manifest in your life. Your own words of deliverance can free you.

Psalms 34:13 says, *"Keep thy tongue from evil, and thy lips from speaking guile."* *Keep* there is the Hebrew word *natsar,* meaning to guard, to protect, or to maintain something, and it means to besiege a city, to put it under siege (Strong, H5341). When an army besieged a city they would surround it; they wouldn't let anybody come in or go out. They maintained the siege as long as the fight continued. Guard your words. Watch what comes out. Be careful with the sentences you connect together. Be careful of the thoughts you are giving life to by your words.

Keep your tongue from evil. The word for "evil" is the Hebrew word *ra,* and it means poor quality or inferior quality (Strong, H7451). It pictures a garment that is flawed. We might call it second best. The Hebrews would say it's *ra*—it has something wrong with it. The psalmist says you can't live a quality Christian life unless you guard your words. Your life will become flawed, poor quality, inferior to the life you could live. If you don't watch your words you're going to have second best.

Then it says to keep your lips from speaking guile. *Guile* is the Hebrew word *mirmah*, meaning to trick or deceive (Strong, H4820). An example of this is a deceptive bait that is used to catch fish. If you go fishing, you might put a night crawler or a crawdad on a hook to deceive the fish. When the fish bites he gets more than he bargained for—he gets hooked, and before he knows it he is caught. Keep your lips from speaking guile. In other words, don't connect sentences together that are going to hook you. Don't take the bait. Don't let hell's kingdom, the world, or anything bait you into declaring something that is going to hook, catch, or trap you. You could be the one who is reeled in and caught. Guard your words.

Guile also applies to deceiving someone else or speaking evil of another. Don't bad-mouth anybody. Scripture says to speak evil of no one. Don't word curse anyone because it will align you with lucifer instead of God. One of the definitions of the name *satan* is "slanderer" (Strong, G1228). When you gossip you're slandering. Gossip is demon language. Satan is the accuser of the brethren, but when you gossip or speak evil of someone you are assisting hell's kingdom. Also, the Word of God warns us that the words you speak against another could put a hook in your jaw, and God promises that the trap you lay for somebody else with the words of your mouth will ruin your quality of life. You are going to ruin yourself doing that. Don't speak guile. Guard your words.

Jesus said you are going to have what you say. Your words of faith in God shall come to pass. They are building blocks—*legos*—to the good quality of life. If you speak your faith you are going to have it. What you say sets in motion what is about to happen and constructs your quality of life. Jesus said what you say you will have. Summon things to you that will bless you. Dispatch things from you that are going to hinder you. Release your authority in Jesus' name.

LINDA'S STORY

I started my day like every other work day, but on this day for some reason I noticed all the beautiful cherry trees on the walkway leading into the entrance. Everything was crisp and refreshing; it was a beautiful spring day. In my office, I began digging into the day's work. Two hours later, I was called into the conference room and a woman from Human Resources informed me that my position had been terminated. As she began talking about severance pay, COBRA, and resources available to me, all I could remember later of the conversation was Charlie Brown's teacher. Nothing she said made sense; it was just blah, blah, blah, and blah.

Severance pay. Strangely enough only a few days later I was listening to a program, and they mentioned the origin of the term. It originated in the middle ages when an executioner was paid to sharpen their blade so the head could be cut off in one swing. That was exactly how I felt. My head had been cut off and I didn't have a clear thought.

As I left the office that day, nothing seemed quite as crisp and fresh as it did earlier. I began going through the motions of looking for a new job. I had acquired my now nonexistent job without a college degree and had worked my way up in the company. Without a degree I was finding it difficult to get employment in the same field. I decided to try to go back to school. I went to the local community college and spoke with a counselor who used to work for Work Force One in my county. As I told him my story, he let me know that in my situation there was a good chance they would pay for my education. God had me in the right place at the right time with the right people. I enrolled in a program that would educate me for a growing field that was in high demand, paid for my books, tuition, and travel expenses to get there and back.

During all of this, my husband and I continued to do what we had always done; we remained in covenant with God, decreeing and declaring His Word in our lives. We continued to give our tithes and offerings. Through all of this it was evident that God's math is better than ours. We never had a moment of lack.

I graduated in 2013, exactly 12 months after my journey began. I passed my exams and achieved my certification and was employed one month later. I received my first paycheck the very week my unemployment ran out. I have received several promotions, and in just three years I am making nearly what it took me 14 years to make in the job that I lost.

We plant the seed and He grows, it if we trust Him.

—Linda Collinsworth

MOUNTAIN
MOVING FAITH

*And when they had come to the multitude, a man came
to Him, kneeling down to Him and saying, "Lord,
have mercy on my son, for he is an epileptic and suffers
severely; for he often falls into the fire and often into
the water. So I brought him to Your disciples, but they
could not cure him." Then Jesus answered and said,
"O faithless and perverse generation, how long shall
I be with you? How long shall I bear with you? Bring
him here to Me." And Jesus rebuked the demon, and
it came out of him; and the child was cured from that
very hour. Then the disciples came to Jesus privately
and said, "Why could we not cast it out?" So Jesus said
to them, "Because of your unbelief; for assuredly, I say
to you, if you have faith as a mustard seed, you will
say to this mountain, 'Move from here to there,' and it
will move; and nothing will be impossible for you."*
—MATTHEW 17:14-20 NKJV

There is a faith that moves mountains, but mountain moving faith often must be grown. That requires perseverance and consistency on our part. Mountains do not move by small faith; they move by great faith that is consistently grown. You move mountains by faith that is maintained, nurtured, and guarded. Faith grows to maturity and produces what is decreed. You change circumstances and situations, not by a faith that is moved by what it sees or how it feels, but by a faith that is moved by the Word of the Living God.

Christ's own words in Luke 12:28, "*O ye of little faith,*" are not an affirmation. They are a correction and a call to grow. Jesus told His disciples to feed the multitude of five thousand. They said, "We can't, there's not enough." "*O ye of little faith*" was Jesus' reply to His disciples (see Matt. 16:8). Then, when the storm rose up on the Sea of Galilee and the disciples started screaming out, "Don't you care that we perish?" He says "*Why are ye so fearful? How is it that ye have no faith?*" (Mark 4:40).

The apostle Peter actually stepped out on the water, saying, "Jesus, if that's really You, bid me come." When Jesus did, Peter walked a few steps, saw the waves, and began to sink. Jesus said to him, "*O ye of little faith, wherefore didst thou doubt?*" (Matt. 14:31). These were words of correction and a call to grow more faith. This is important to understand because the word of faith we decree is often tested by difficult and stormy times. There may be times when the waves are high and you think you are going to sink or times when you lack the faith needed to accomplish the job. If you have been saved for any period of time, you have probably been tested by life conditions. Most people have had their faith tested by situations where it looked like what was happening was the opposite of what was decreed. And the fight of faith is on.

In 1998, I was studying Matthew 17:14-20. I was trying to get some understanding concerning some very difficult situations. I had dealt with several tragedies that had occurred, I was burying people who were way too young, and it was testing my faith. My reasoning was asking questions like the disciples asked: "Why? What's going on?" Often, tragedy or loss can cause you to put your nose in the Book and begin to search for answers—that's a good thing. I felt like my faith was not working, and I really didn't know what to do about it. It seemed like what I believed was being challenged. My faith felt kind of numb, even though I trusted God. I wanted to serve and do what I could for Him, but there were prayers that I had been praying that weren't being answered.

As I read Matthew 17, a valuable principle and a very freeing truth began to be revealed. I began to see faith differently than the way I had been taught as a young boy in Sunday school. Overcoming mountains isn't always easy. Some situations that come your way challenge you to the core of who you really are. A little bit of faith is not all you need. For the first time, I began to see faith as a seed that could grow and meet the challenge of a mountain.

This particular principle confronted me, but at the same time it freed me to move to a higher level of confidence and faith to see signs, wonders, miracles, and prayers answered. This passage revealed *growing faith* to me. I heard Holy Spirit say, "You need to grow your faith," and I began to see some things I hadn't considered before. I had to plant faith with my words aligned with God's Word so it could grow to challenge and overcome the mountain.

That simple challenge by Holy Spirit was not said to me with any condemnation at all. I had asked for an answer and I received one. It was said in love and grace, but it was unmistakable. "You need to grow your faith." That simple answer of the Holy Spirit challenged me and inspired me to move my life into ever increasing faith.

A man came to Jesus with his son who was in real trouble. The boy was suicidal. The King James says he was a lunatic and he was out of his head. The child kept throwing himself into the fire trying to commit suicide. You can imagine, if you were the parent of a child like that you would have to watch them all the time. This was a horrible situation. The man told Jesus he brought his son to the disciples who prayed over him, but nothing happened. So the man decided to bring his son to Jesus. We are told that Jesus rebuked the evil spirit that was tormenting this child, set him free, and he was absolutely totally healed from that moment on. Of course, that changed the life of that family. It was a tremendous miracle that Jesus accomplished.

Later on the disciples came privately to Jesus and said, "Why couldn't we take care of this? Why couldn't we drive that spirit out and heal that child?" Jesus answered them, "It's because of your unbelief." I have often wondered what they thought or how they felt when He said that to them. With some Christians that wouldn't go over so well. *Unbelief* is the Greek word *apistia,* and it means unfaithfulness, mistrust, lack of faith, little or small faith, negative belief, uncertainty, lack of confidence in power, and to hesitate (Strong, G570). Jesus said to them, "It's because of your unbelief, your negative belief." In other words, you do believe; you just believed nothing was going to happen, so that's what happened. Your lack of faith kept you from seeing a miracle. Negative belief kept it from happening. Your negative thought processes stopped the promise that I had given to you. Your lack of confidence in My power kept prayer for this boy from being effective. Jesus clearly says that unbelief will stop miracles from happening. Uncertainty will stop prayers from being answered. Mistrust of Christ's power keeps demon powers engaged. Little faith stifles promises that He has made to you. Negative belief allows demons to continue to operate.

More than likely some of you have been in a similar situation. You have prayed for things that didn't happen. The miracle desired did not occur. You prayed but demon activity continued, the mountain didn't move, those you prayed for were not healed, and you find yourself asking the same question the disciples asked, "Why? Why didn't it happen?" It's sometimes hard to accept Christ's answer that it is because faith is too small. Yes, faith was present—He acknowledges that, but it was small. So when challenged in your thinking by real conditions, your confidence faltered at the size of the mountain and you hesitated at the point where power needed to be released to change things—just like the disciples. Sometimes we have difficulty accepting that there could be areas of unbelief in us, but Jesus teaches that there can be areas where we lack faith and our faith is small.

We often use religious excuses instead of making corrections. For example, "Well, it's not God's will, the timing is off, or I'm just in the wrong place, I need to switch churches or something." Many have prayed for something with a nagging feeling of uncertainty inside of them that it's not going to work. They hope it does, but they feel uncertain (*apistia*). They are hoping but they are not trusting. Hope is a good thing—without it we are miserable. Hope gives peace and rest in our emotions. But hope only affects you and your soul; it doesn't affect the mountain—faith does.

Please understand that these disciples had faith. They weren't completely faithless; they just lacked the faith it took to change this situation. Remember, in Matthew 10 Jesus gave them power to heal the sick and to cast out demons. Then He sent them out two by two to do that, and they reported back to Him, "It worked. Our faith in Your promise to us actually worked. We saw the sick healed, and even demons were subject to us. We saw tremendous miracles. Our faith produced." But by Matthew 17 they came to a situation where they lacked the faith they needed to change it. Clearly, you can have faith one day and be in unbelief the next.

Please understand, they still had the same authority that Jesus had given to them over demon spirits and the same ability to heal the sick. Jesus had not taken back the authority that He had given to them. They had seen their faith work, but this time uncertainty came in. Evidently they had not been maintaining their faith, keeping it nurtured and fresh inside of them. Possibly it was human reasoning that eroded it. Maybe it was what they saw with their natural eyes because it was a difficult situation they were facing. It could have been the negative belief system of the people all around them that eroded it or fear that brought the uncertainty. Perhaps it was pride in their former accomplishments, as though they had done it instead of Christ's power. Maybe they just talked themselves out of it, saying, "We know it worked last time, but who is to say it's going to work this time?" Obviously, someone in their group injected negativity into the scenario.

They forgot the basic tenet of apostolic doctrine—faith needs to be maintained, nurtured with God's Word, guarded against any negativity, and kept alive and growing. This is what Jesus was teaching here in this passage. What He said next is one of the most misunderstood statements in New Testament Scripture. Jesus does not say that it just takes a little bit of faith to move a mountain. He does not say, "Just have small faith and nothing will be impossible to you." He's not advocating for tiny faith in His people. He had just corrected His disciples for having faith that was too small and didn't get the job done. *The Message* reads, "How many times do I have to go over this? Focus."

I think I have heard Him say that statement to me a few times. He's not saying, "Just keep a tiny little bit of faith in you, about the size of a mustard seed, so you can move mountains and see the impossible done." That really doesn't make any sense because it takes a whole lot more faith and power to move a mountain than it does a molehill.

Yet many think that this is what He meant, and when the mountain doesn't move and when faith is challenged and the situation does not change they think, "I must not even have a mustard seed size of faith. Why should I pray at all? I must not have any faith at all." That isn't true! You do have faith, just like the disciples had faith. In fact, every Christian has been given a measure of faith: *"God has dealt to every man the measure of faith"* (Rom. 12:3). Jesus is saying faith should be alive and growing. He is talking about a faith that is living.

"And Jesus said unto them, Because of your unbelief: for verily I say unto you, If ye have faith as a grain of mustard seed, ye shall say unto this mountain, Remove hence to yonder place; and it shall remove; and nothing shall be impossible unto you" (Matt. 17:20). Notice, He does not use the word *size*. He doesn't say faith the "size" of a mustard seed; this changes the meaning dramatically. He says "as." *As* is the Greek word *hos,* and it means in the manner of or in the way of (Strong, G5613). The word for "faith" is the Greek word *pistis,* which means trust, confidence, certainty, to be persuaded, and conviction that is not based upon sight or knowledge (Strong, G4102). It is not based on what I see, how I feel, or what reason may be saying to me—it's based upon what God says:

> He answered, "Because of your little faith [your lack of trust and confidence in the power of God]; for I assure you and most solemnly say to you, if you have [living] faith the size of a mustard seed, you will say to this mountain, 'Move from here to there,' and [if it is God's will] it will move; and nothing will be impossible for you" (Matthew 17:20 AMP).

He says faith is living, alive, and growing. A seed isn't active; it's asleep. It isn't growing; it's in a state of dormancy. A seed is a potential harvest that is not activated yet. Words are what activate the seeds. You have to plant your faith with words that align with God's Word and then keep your confession of faith consistent, keep those word seed decrees free of unbelief. They will produce harvest. They will produce after their kind. They will grow up to where they can overcome a mountain. The DNA of the seed you plant will then sprout, bud, and grow to fullness. Plant words of faith and keep them growing. Sow words of faith that will lay a foundation for good life, and don't negate them. Plant God's Word and let it grow to move mountains. Activate your faith and keep it alive.

Jesus is not saying, "Have dormant faith like seeds that are asleep." That wouldn't make any sense. He is talking about faith as a grain of mustard seed that has been planted and is alive and growing. It's been decreed, not negated, and kept alive. If your faith grows in the manner of a mustard seed, then it will move mountains. The parallel passage to this in Mark 4 gives more clarity:

> And he said, Whereunto shall we liken the kingdom of God? or with what comparison shall we compare it? It is like a grain of mustard seed, which, when it is sown in the earth, is less than all the seeds that be in the earth: but when it is sown, it groweth up, and becometh greater than all herbs, and shooteth out great branches; so that the fowls of the air may lodge under the shadow of it (Mark 4:30-32).

It grows up. *Grows up* is the Greek word *anabaino,* and it means to arise, to spring up, or to ascend (Strong, G305). *Ana* is the Greek word for up, to climb up, to climb higher, or ascend up. *Baino* is a word meaning to go or to move up higher or go to a different level. Jesus is talking about a faith that grows up. It's a faith that is alive. It's growing, maturing, and kept that way. He said to His disciples, "Here's why your faith did not work. It was too little. But it's like a mustard seed. You need to plant it and grow it some more. You need to get it living in you. You need to declare it. And you need to keep it nurtured. You need to keep it moving on up. You need to mature it. It's not where it needs to be—move it up. Grow it some more."

Sometimes we face a situation and our faith is just too small to handle it. We need faith to change it. What do you do? Jesus said you grow it! You go to work on your faith and you move it up. You soak your heart in what God says, and you keep doing that while your faith grows. You say what God says and refuse to negate it.

Jesus also taught there were different levels of faith. He said there is little faith, small faith, and great faith. He taught that faith can grow or be brought to higher levels. It can go from tiny to small to large as you grow it. But He never taught that small faith would move mountains.

Thirty-six years ago we were trying to buy our first church building. We had outgrown our first building and had the opportunity to purchase a small church. I will never forget how I felt inside when they said the payment was going to be three hundred dollars a month. It might as well have been three thousand. We had nothing. I thought, "We can't do three hundred dollars. We are struggling to do this. What do we do?"

I remember preaching a sermon on Jehovah Jireh, God our Provider, and I listed all these Scriptures about how God blesses and sends prosperity. I began to soak myself in those Scriptures and ponder them. I began to declare them every morning, afternoon, and every time I thought about it. I started declaring what God said and I started to grow my faith. Certainty started to come: "We can do this. We can do it. We can conquer this." I know it sounds really small now, but it wasn't then. Amazingly, we were able to pay that building off in less than a year.

We outgrew that building and then we went to Central School. What's the payment on that one? Fifteen hundred a month. Oh wow. Felt it again, "That's impossible. We can't do that. We're not even close. We can't do it." But again, Jehovah Jireh is our Provider. I went back to the Book and I began to soak myself again in what God says: "God, You make a way when there's no way. You send prosperity. You meet all of our needs." Soak yourself in the Word and you're growing your faith to a different level. I began to do that and we stepped out by faith, signed the contract, and began to move in. While we were moving in, an elderly lady came in and said, "Pastor, how much do we have to pay on this?"

I said, "Fifteen hundred a month."

She pulled out a check and said, "Here's the first year. Go do it." She paid for the whole year! An $18,000 check. My faith had to grow. We had to step out and take that act of faith and believe.

We outgrew that building and then purchased land to build a new sanctuary. What's the payment? Seven thousand five hundred. Oh wow. It might as well have been seven million. How in the world can you pay that every month? What do you do? You do what the Word says. Soak yourself in the Word and say what God says. You begin to believe and grow your faith. This is not too hard for God. Jehovah Jireh is our Provider. Again, we had to grow a faith that would enable us to meet the challenge.

Soon we had outgrown this building and had to have a larger one, the one we're in now. During this process the economy went into a recession and changed everything. What should have been manageable became temporarily impossible in the natural. Again, wow, we had to grow our faith. We began to declare what God says, and He began to do miracles. He was Jehovah Jireh, so gracious and so kind, and He helped us financially many times. We grew our faith to meet the mountain.

The point is, faith for three hundred dollars thirty-six years ago wouldn't get it done today. It's too small. Faith has had to grow.

Thankfully, God has blessed, and to God be all the glory. We had to stretch our faith and confidence in God that nothing is too hard for Him, even though initially I thought there was no way.

If faith isn't kept alive and growing, it goes into dormancy. Uncertainty comes and we find ourselves facing situations that do not change, and we wonder why when we saw victories in our past by faith. Like the disciples, we need to remember that faith needs to be maintained, guarded, matured, and kept alive. Keep it healthy. As Christ's disciples, we never mature beyond the need to water the seed with God's Word. You water it, feed it, confess it, and declare it to move it to a higher level.

Governor Mario Cuomo of New York wrote one of my favorite stories in *Life Magazine* years ago. It was about a time in his own life when he was very discouraged over a political campaign that he was in. It says this:

> I couldn't help wondering what Poppa would have said if I told him I was tired or—God forbid—discouraged. A thousand pictures flashed through my mind, but one scene came sharply into view.
>
> We had just moved to Holliswood, New York, from our apartment behind the store. We had our own house for the first time; it had some land around it, even trees. One in particular was a great blue spruce that must have been forty feet tall.
>
> Less than a week after we moved in, there was a terrible storm. We came home from the store that night to find the spruce pulled almost totally from the ground and flung forward, its mighty nose bent in the asphalt of the street. My brother Frankie and I could climb poles all day; we were great at fire escapes; we could scale fences with

barbed wire—but we knew nothing about trees. When we saw our spruce, defeated, its cheek on the canvas, our hearts sank. But not Poppa's.

Maybe he was five feet six if his heels were not worn. Maybe he weighed 155 pounds if he had a good meal. Maybe he could see a block away if his glasses were clean. But he was stronger than Frankie and me and Maria and Momma all together. We stood in the street, looking down at the tree.

"OK, we gonna push 'im up!"

"What are you talking about, Poppa? The roots are out of the ground!"

"Shut up, we gonna push 'im up, he's gonna grow again." You couldn't say no to him. So we followed him into the house and we got what rope there was and we tied the rope around the tip of the tree that lay in the asphalt, and he stood up by the house, with me pulling on the rope and Frankie in the street in the rain, helping to push up the great blue spruce. In no time at all, we had it standing up straight again!

With the rain still falling, Poppa dug away at the place where the roots were, making a muddy hole wider and wider as the tree sank lower and lower toward security. Then we shoveled mud over the roots and moved boulders to the base to keep the tree in place. Poppa drove stakes in the ground, tied rope from the trunk to the stakes, and maybe two hours later looked at the spruce, the crippled spruce made straight by ropes, and said, "Don't worry, he's gonna grow again..."

If you were to drive past that house today, you would see the great, straight blue spruce, maybe sixty-five feet tall, pointing up to the heavens, pretending it never had its nose in the asphalt.[1]

Anabaino. You have to push it up. If your faith is down, if it's small, you're going to have to push it up. Get your nose off the ground and push it up. Declare, "I'm going to grow again. I'm going to grow some more."

In 1952, Sir Edmund Hillary attempted to climb Mt. Everest, the highest peak on earth—29,000 feet above sea level. A few weeks after the expedition failed to climb Mt. Everest, he was asked to address a group of people in England. Sir Edmund Hillary walked up to speak, and at the edge of the stage he made a fist and he pointed at a picture of Mt. Everest. He said to that picture in a very loud voice, "Mt. Everest, you beat me the first time, but I'm going to beat you the next time because you've grown all you're going to grow but I'm still growing." On May 29, 1953, one year later, Sir Edmund Hillary became the first man to ever climb Mt. Everest.[2]

The mountain is as big as it's going to get, but you're still growing. Your faith can still grow. You can outgrow it. Move it up. *Anabaino.* Grow your faith to another level until you beat it, and then use that deeper faith. It may be turbulent, it may be dangerous, but you can grow your faith to a level that anchors you. You can grow it to move a mountain.

Ben Patterson, a mountain climber, writes about a time back in 1988 when he and three of his friends were climbing Mt. Lyell, the highest peak in Yosemite National Park. Their base camp was 2,000 feet from the top of Mt. Lyell, and from that base camp it would take them approximately all day long to get to the top because they had to cross a large glacier. On the day of the climb the two more experienced climbers opened up a large gap between Ben and his climbing partner, who were less experienced. Ben, being very competitive in his nature, began to look for a shortcut so he could beat them to the top. He saw what he thought was a shortcut just to the right of an outcropping of rock so he went that way. His companion protested, but he just kept going. He writes this:

> Perhaps it was the effect of the high altitude, but the significance of the two experienced climbers not choosing this path did not register on my conscience. It should have, for thirty minutes later, I was trapped in a cul-de-sac of rock atop the Lyell glacier, looking down several hundred feet of sheer slope of ice, pitched at a forty-five degree angle. ...I was only about ten feet from the safety of a rock, but one little slip and I wouldn't stop sliding until I landed in the valley floor some fifty miles away. It was nearly noon, the warm sun had the glacier glistening with slippery ice, and I was scared. It took an hour for my experienced climbing friends to find me.
>
> Standing on the rock I wanted to reach, one of them leaned out and used an ice axe to chip two little footsteps into the glacier. Then he gave me the following instructions, "Ben, you must step out from where you are and put your foot where the first foothold is. When your foot touches it, without a moment's hesitation swing your other foot across and land it on the next step. When you do that, reach out and I will take your hand and pull you to safety."
>
> That sounded good to me; it was the next thing he said that made me more frightened than ever. "Listen carefully," he said, "as you step across, do not lean into the mountain. If anything, lean out a bit. Otherwise, your feet may fly out from under you and you will start sliding down."
>
> I don't like precipices. When I am on the edge of the cliff my instincts are to lie down and hug the mountain,

to become one with it, not to lean away from it. But that was what my good friend was telling me to do. ...For a moment, based solely on what I believed to be true about the good will and good sense of my friend, I decided to say no to what I felt, to stifle my impulse to cling to the security of the mountain, to lean out, step out, and traverse the ice to safety. It took less than two seconds to find out if my faith was well-founded. It was.[3]

Sometimes you've got to say no to how you feel and what your own reasoning is telling you to cling to. Sometimes you've got to grow your faith, stepping out and trusting what God says. To safely overcome the mountains that are before you, you have to lean not on your own understanding. You have to step out in faith. At various points in life, we all find ourselves either living in the potential of our faith or the consequences of our doubt. Determine to live in the potential of your faith.

NOTES

1. Edward K. Rowell, *1001 Quotes, Illustrations, and Humorous Stories for Preachers, Teachers, and Writers* (Grand Rapids, MI: Baker Books, 2008), 243-244.

2. At Boshoff, *Live a Yes Life: Become All That You Possibly Can Be* (Cape Town: Struik Christian Books, 2008), 83.

3. Ben Patterson, *Waiting: Finding Hope When God Seems Silent* (Downers Grove, IL: InterVarsity Press, 1989).

CHAPTER

12

THE MANIFESTO

THIS MEANS WAR

During an extended time of praise and worship, I had a vision of two submarines—one very old, the other more modern. As the older submarine plunged under the water, the Holy Spirit spoke: "This is the charismatic church that is now submerged into what she once influenced." The other, newer model was a nuclear and mighty battle ship. When it surfaced on the water, the Holy Spirit declared, "This is My remnant church that is going to rule and reign with Me." I thought, *Praise God, we are going nuclear.*

America, our government, and our judicial system are in a mess. Our schools and many of our churches are in a mess. The American culture and a troubled economy are in crisis. America certainly needs awakening and reformation, and if we are going to see it in our lifetime, the church must understand its mandate and how to achieve it. Determined to turn the soul of our nation back to the principles upon which it was founded, I began to ponder New Testament, apostolic war statements.

Prompted by the Holy Spirit, I began extensive, in-depth studies on the New Testament church, reformation, spiritual warfare, and their relationship in conjunction with reformation. It did not take long to recognize the pattern that was developing. I began to see a *Christian warrior's manifesto* that the apostle Paul consistently talked about. A *manifesto* is a published verbal declaration of the intentions, motives, or views of an individual, group, political party, or government. Words are powerful enough to inspire movements, which is why we plant the heavens with word seed decrees. One of the greatest word seed decrees is the apostle Paul's manifesto.

> For though we walk in the flesh, we do not war after the flesh. For the weapons of our warfare are not carnal but mighty in God for pulling down strongholds (2 Corinthians 10:3-4 NKJV).

He says very clearly there is a war, we have weapons, and there are strongholds that we are supposed to pull down. The word for "war" is the Greek word *strateuomai,* and it means to serve in a military campaign (Strong, G4754). Uniquely, it is a word used only in the first-century church of Paul's day, referring to an apostolate. An apostolate, a New Testament church, is one that is actively releasing the five-fold ministry of apostles, prophets, evangelists, pastors, and teachers as listed in Ephesians 4:11. Literally, *war* means to execute the plans and purposes of a New Testament church. Jude tells us to contend for the faith—the original faith that was delivered to us, not what it has morphed into today.

God is building an angel-assisted New Testament church that will be able to execute the five-fold ministry and perform as soldiers in an apostolate. The early church considered it a privileged duty to execute and extend the strategies of Heaven in their region. It was not forced rhetoric but privileged obedience. What would happen today if millions considered it an honor to execute and extend Holy Spirit-prompted strategies to reform culture in their regions through apostolates? Like the early church, they would evangelize this world for Kingdom of God purposes. Get this in your spirit—it is your Christian duty and critical to the soul of this nation to enforce the principles of God through your apostolate. The first step toward reformation is embracing a sense of duty. Somewhere, that sense of duty has gotten lost.

And having a readiness to revenge all disobedience, when your obedience is fulfilled (2 Corinthians 10:6).

Readiness is the Greek word *hetoimos,* and it means to be fit, prepared, and ready (Strong, G2092). "To revenge" is the Greek word *ekdikeo,* meaning to vindicate, retaliate, enforce, punish, avenge (Strong, G1556). The word for "disobedience" is the Greek word *parakoe,* and it means to hear the wrong words or to carelessly hear wrong things that lead to disobedience (Strong, G3876). When you repeatedly listen to wrong words it can lead to disobedience individually or corporately. Our minds are fashioned negatively, and this causes our actions to be in error. We cannot allow the adversary to frame our language to fit his motives.

The apostle Paul says an apostolate must be ready to retaliate with decrees of faith to plant the heavens until faith is sowed into the earth. His message implores believers to be fit and ready to enforce what God says—to be active warriors and to fight for what is divine. Clearly the apostolic call is for aggressive Christianity and not passive appeasement. Winston Churchill said of those who seek to appease their enemies, "Each one hopes that if he feeds the crocodile enough, the crocodile will eat him last." We are here to challenge disobedience with truth.

"Obedience" is the Greek word *hupakoe,* meaning to obey, hearken, listen attentively to, comply, and submit to the will of God (Strong, G5218). It also appears in First Peter 1:22, referring to obedience to the truth. "Fulfilled" is the Greek word *pleroo,* and it means to complete, accomplish, finish, or perform (Strong, G4137). Paul also uses it in Romans 15:19 to refer to manifesting the Christian faith. Visibly show your faith. What a powerful New Testament statement being declared by the apostle Paul!

The original language of Second Corinthians 10:3-6 is so powerful. Hear it as originally intended: "Submit and comply to the will of God, manifesting your Christian faith by being fit and ready to enforce and avenge words contrary to God's words. Be actively engaged warriors, prepared to retaliate when necessary and always ready to extend completely and fully through your own obedience the strategies of your apostolates that pull down enemy strongholds. Be engaged and ready at all times to execute your Christian duties with aggressive faith."

What a statement. Certainly the New Testament church in Colossae, Corinth, Ephesus, and in Philippi understood that they were at war. They did not have their heads buried in the sand as many in the Body of Christ do today. They understood they were to be engaged warriors—warriors who retaliated and avenged. They fought for what was right, and they engaged in their culture. But in our times we have lost that sense of duty. We've lost the warrior's mentality, and we have allowed the world to define us. We cannot allow the world to define us. We must have God and His Word define us.

DOMINION MANDATE

From the world's view, Christians are supposed to be peaceful and loving and turn the other cheek. Personally, I will turn the other cheek when wronged, but I will not turn my cheek to cultural sin and disobedience to God's Word. We are never told to, nor will I, submit to ungodliness. We want peace, but not at the exclusion of contending for God's principles. Paul is very consistent in his teaching concerning warfare against antichrist cultural or societal conditions in the world because he themes it throughout most of his writings, as do the other apostles, especially Jude and the apostle Peter.

In Ephesians 5:11-12, Paul issues very aggressive warfare commands. These Scriptures are written to frontline soldiers equipped by the five-fold ministry. They are not written to someone who pacifies or appeases their opposition. He then moves to Ephesians 6 and gives the ekklesia another very aggressive command. It is a command that we must engage in our times: *"Finally, my brethren, be strong in the Lord, and in the power of his might"* (Eph. 6:10). "Finally" is the descriptive word *loipon* in the Greek language, and though it is the first word of the statement, it does not mean "lastly." We need to focus on what Paul is trying to convey to us here. *Loipon* means something remaining, remaining ones, or a remnant (Strong, G3063). You almost have to shout this text to read it correctly. "Remnant warriors; those who do not run; those who do not quit; those who do not scatter, those who stand; those who remain, those who make a stand." The apostle Paul begins with a declaration to remnant warriors—to the Triumphant Reserve. He exhorts, "Be strong, remnant ones; be strong, remnant warriors."

Our military today has soldiers in the regular army, but it also has Special Forces units. We have Army Rangers and Navy Seals. They are "bad to the bone" dudes. Don't mess with them. *Loipon* is the word for the special forces units of the Kingdom of God. They are "bad to the bone" spiritual warfare soldiers. Don't mess with them because they are engaging themselves through a Kingdom ekklesia.

Shortly after beginning this word study, one of our intercessors approached me with a dream she had. At the end of the dream, she heard the Holy Spirit speak the word *systema*. Having no idea what it meant, I searched for a similar Greek word but found nothing. We would have to rely solely on God to reveal whatever was hidden in this word. Here is some history of *systema*. The root of it is based in the Russian Orthodox Christian faith, and is nearly 100 years old. Today, a form of Russian Martial Arts is called Systema.

> Throughout the history of this huge country, Russia had to repel invaders from the north, south, east, and west. All attackers brought their distinct styles of combat and weaponry. The battles took place on different terrain, during freezing winters and sweltering summer heat alike, with the Russians often greatly outnumbered by the enemy forces. As a result of these factors, the Russian warriors acquired a style that combined strong spirit with extremely innovative and versatile tactics that were at the same time practical, deadly, and effective against any type of enemy under any circumstances. The style was natural and free while having no strict rules, rigid structure or limitations (except for moral ones). All tactics were based on instinctive reactions, individual strengths and characteristics, specifically designed for fast learning.[1]

In 1917, the Communist Party thought to do away with this training, thinking it harmful to their control, but the Christians kept it alive. Today, the Systema are some of the best-trained special forces in the world. They are fearless, bold, faithful, and committed to their cause. The Systema are the elite forces. Here is what they do:

- They work high-risk missions.
- They are trained in an ancient style fighting passed down through the generations.
- They can fight any style of war.

- They are trained in modern weapons of war and constantly update their uses.

- They are taught to defend themselves from attack from any direction.

- They are trained in disarming weapons and weapon systems.

- They are trained to improvise and fight in nontraditional situations (such as sitting in a chair).

- They are taught to use whatever comes to hand with deadly force.

- They are trained to relax before they strike rather than adopt a fierce countenance so they can strike from unusual angles.

- They are taught to smile in combat.

The purpose for this discipline is to improve their mental state, to operate without stress in a stress-filled environment, to be at peace when under attack, and to relax tension in the body so they are limber enough to strike in all directions.

I believe the Lord's Systema is now emerging on the earth—those who will smile when under attack; those who will relax and be at peace and yet attack hell in all directions; those who will fight hell's kingdom on any terrain, any time, any place. Those who are not afraid of some high-risk missions; those who will fight in nontraditional situations. They will fight with God's morals, but understand that the Systema is relentless in battle and they intend to win. We need to hold fast a determination to finish for the cause of Jesus Christ.

Paul says, "Remnant warriors, *loipon*, special forces units in the Kingdom of God, be strong in the Lord and in the power of His might." *Lord* is the Greek word *kyrios*, meaning master, superintendent, controller, and supreme in authority (Strong, G2962). So be strong in the supreme authority of the Lord. Be strong in the Master's delegated authority. Remnant warriors, superintend and control with your authority.

Power is the Greek word *kratos*, meaning to manifest evident force, activated forces, and dominion (Strong, G2904). This is Paul's reference to the dominion mandate in Genesis 1:26-28 when God commands man to have dominion over every living thing and subdue the earth. Paul is calling for the remnant to dominate with Christ's supreme authority. It's part of your Christian duty.

Might is the Greek word *ischus*, and it means ability, capacity, prevail (Strong, G2479). Paul says be strong in the Lord's abilities that are freely delegated to you. Move in His capacities, prevailing, superintending, and dominating principalities, powers, mights, and dominions. Rise up within your apostolates and dominate demons. Paul would have been hard-pressed to use stronger language.

LOIPON, KURIUS, ISCHUS

"Remnant warriors, be strong in the prevailing capacities of your Lord, dominating, superintending, and controlling with God's abilities manifesting through you over the powers of hell. Don't run, quit, or scatter; stand, remain, and in Jesus' name dominate demons." Clearly, retreat was not on Paul's mind. He is a spiritual general rallying warriors.

"Put on the whole armour of God, that ye may be able to stand against the wiles of the devil" (Eph. 6:11). The Greek words Paul uses here are, again, bold and commanding. "Be able" is the Greek word *dunamis*, meaning can do, possible, can-do possibility, to have power, to have resources (Strong, G1410/1411). It is possible, and you do have powers against the wiles of the devil through delegated authority from Christ.

You are here to dominate hell, not tolerate it. You are here to make a stand.

"Stand" is the Greek word *histemi*, meaning to make a stand (Strong, G2476). "Against" is the word *pro*, meaning to step forward, to march forward, to march with purpose (Strong, G4314). "Wiles" is the Greek word *methodeia*, meaning method, arts, cunning devices, craftiness, and procedures (Strong, G3180). As he leads up to wearing armor, hear what General Paul, the apostle, says in context with Second Corinthians 10 and Ephesians 6:

> *Submit and comply to the will of God, manifesting your Christian faith by being fit and ready to enforce and avenge words contrary to God's words and laws contrary to God's laws. Be actively engaged warriors prepared to retaliate when necessary and always ready to extend completely and fully through your own obedience the strategies of your Kingdom ekklesia that pull down your enemy's strongholds. Be engaged and ready at all times to execute your Christian duties with aggressive faith.*
>
> *Remnant warriors, be strong in the prevailing capacities of your Lord, dominating, superintending, regulating, and controlling with God's abilities manifesting through you over the powers of hell. Do not run, quit, or scatter. Never flinch. Stand, remain, and in Jesus' name dominate demons because you have been given can-do power in Christ's name to step forward on purpose and with purpose and make a stand against demon methods, against demon devices, and all demon procedures whether they be political, governmental, religious, or idolatrous. Therefore, put your armor on and march forward. March toward the wiles of the devil; march, march, march; I said march.*

WARRIOR'S MANIFESTO

For You have armed me with strength for the battle; You have subdued under me those who rose against me (2 Samuel 22:40 NKJV).

In that day the Lord of hosts will be for a crown of glory and a diadem of beauty to the remnant of His people, for a spirit of justice to him who sits in judgment, and for strength to those who turn back the battle at the gate (Isaiah 28:5-6 NKJV).

In Bible days, the city gate was like our nation's capital, Washington, D.C., or a state capital such as Columbus for Ohio. Business was transacted at the gate. Legislation was enacted at the gate. The ekklesia is to take the battle to the gate of our country.

Many say that the church of Jesus Christ has no business in government. They insist you cannot legislate righteousness, yet all the while they are surely and visibly continuing to legislate unrighteousness. Wrongly, the church's thinking for the past 75 years or more has been to stay out of the gates. *Do not involve yourselves in the laws of the land in which you live. Stay in your irrelevant churches and leave the establishing of codes of moral conduct up to the world. Just keep hibernating. We will wake you when winter is over. You are too ignorant and narrow-minded, too dependent and needy to be effective anyway.* Sadly, we have complied, and most are idly watching while the world tramples our Holy God's principles. We have succumbed and hibernated instead of dominating.

David, King of Israel, was one of God's greatest warriors, and he governed and made laws. Still, he was a man after God's own heart, and he had God's approval. Moses was a lawgiver establishing ethical codes of conduct, laws, and penalties for societal violations. The

Book of Judges is about the judges who governed and yet were great men and women of God. Solomon, Deborah, Hezekiah, Gideon, Joseph, Joshua, Saul, Josiah, and Daniel influenced government as well as moral and civic laws or codes of conduct. Esther and Mordecai rewrote laws and prophesied into their government to influence moral and civic laws and codes of conduct. Elijah, Elisha, Samuel, Jeremiah, Isaiah, Nathan, Nehemiah, Hosea, Amos, Obadiah, Ezekiel, Micah, and John the Baptist also did. Paul spoke to leaders and governors of Rome. Stephen, James, and Peter did as well. Where in the world did we get the notion that we are to stay out of the government? It is demon doctrine meant to muzzle the church and kill America as well as others nations of the world. The church is expected to be present at the regional and national gates addressing leaders, governors, and presidents in a manner that brings glory to God.

Clearly our call is to attack the powers of hell through prayer and faith decrees. Followers of Christ are here to war against hell's leadership and to stop its business in the earth today. David tells us in Psalms 60:12 that with God's help we will do mighty things because He will trample down our enemies. Our Lord says he will build His church and the gates of hell will not prevail against it (see Matt. 16:18).

Continuing in Matthew 16:19, Jesus says whatever you bind on earth will be bound in Heaven; whatever you loose on earth will be loosed in Heaven. He will give us supernatural keys for this—the keys of the Kingdom of Heaven. So hit your knees, take His Word, make decrees, and boldly go to war against the powers of darkness. In Him we have power over demons.

Remember, Matthew 16:18 paraphrased from the Greek text reads, "Whatever you at any time encounter of hell's counsel that I am determined My church will prevail against, you will then face a decision as to whether you will or will not bind it. What transpires is conditional to your response. If you do actively and consciously involve yourself in binding the issue on earth, you will find at that future moment when you do that I have bound it in Heaven."

In other words, we have a responsibility to respond aggressively against some things. We're not supposed to be in favor of everything. Consider Ephesians 6:10-12. Paul said the word *against* four times when associated with principalities, powers, the rulers of the darkness of this world, and spiritual wickedness in high places. The word for "against" is the Greek *pro*, as stated earlier. Paul is saying, "Remnant warriors, if you encounter principalities, step forward; don't back up, don't march in place. Step forward. If you see powers, step forward. And if you see spiritual wickedness in high places (which refers to the leadership of hell itself, lucifer), don't back down. You have dominating authority over him; step forward. Rule and reign with the King. In Him is the strength for warfare."

We don't need strength to show off how spiritual we are in front of other people or churches. We need strength for war. A tribal chief once met a very muscular weight lifter. The tribal chief asked, "What do you do?" So the weight lifter struck a pose to better display his muscular physique. "What else do you do?" asked the chief. Again, the weight lifter struck a different pose to give the chief a better view of his muscles. In the end, the tribal chief said, "That's it? What a waste!" That being said, he walked away. Understand that the strength that God gives us is not for some kind of spiritual style show, but it is strength to do battle for Him at the gates. The church is the strongest force on earth. That strength must be used as God intended. We cannot waste it.

THE REMNANT WARRIOR'S MANIFESTO

The Greek words and phrases Paul used unlock a revelation that speaks Holy Spirit enlightenment to us. Once again, please hear the Remnant Warrior's Manifesto:

Submit and comply to the will of God, manifesting your Christian faith by being fit and ready to enforce and avenge words contrary to God's words and laws contrary to God's laws. Be actively engaged warriors prepared to retaliate when necessary and always ready to extend completely and fully through your own obedience the strategies of your Kingdom ekklesia that pull down your enemy's strongholds. Be engaged and ready at all times to execute your Christian duties with aggressive faith.

Remnant warriors, be strong in the prevailing capacities of your Lord, dominating, superintending, regulating, and controlling with God's abilities manifesting through you over the powers of hell. Do not run, quit, or scatter. Never flinch. Stand, remain, and in Jesus' name dominate demons because you have been given can-do power in Christ's name to step forward on purpose and with purpose and make a stand against demon methods, against demon devices, and all demon procedures whether they be political, governmental, religious, or idolatrous. Therefore, put your armor on and march forward. March toward the wiles of the devil; march, march, march; I said march.

So when the enemy comes against you, relax, smile, be at peace and strike hell in all directions. Hallelujah.

PRAYER

Let the remnant emerge. Lord, grant that great boldness be poured out on the remnant across the United States of America and the world. Let the remnant begin to step forward and march into their culture. Release upon us fresh demon-destroying anointing. Let aggressive, visible faith begin to rise.

We declare we will stand. We will change America and turn this world around. We will see revival everywhere. We will fight until we win and see reformation in Jesus' name.

NOTE

1. Vladimir Vasiliev, "What Is Systema?" Russian Martial Art, accessed February 19, 2017, http://www.russianmartialart.com/whatis.php.

About the Author

Dr. Tim Sheets is an apostle, pastor, author, and founder of AwakeningNow Prayer Network based in Middletown, Ohio at the Oasis Church, which he has pastored for 37 years. He travels and ministers across the nation and other countries.

@TimDSheets (Twitter)
Tim Sheets (Facebook)

Tim Sheets Ministries

6927 Lefferson Road
Middletown, Ohio 45044
carol@timsheets.org
513-424-7150

timsheets.org
oasiswired.org
awakeningnowprayernetwork.com

FREE E-BOOKS?
YES, PLEASE!

Get **FREE** and deeply discounted **Christian books** for your **e-reader** delivered to your inbox **every week!**

IT'S SIMPLE!

VISIT lovetoreadclub.com

SUBSCRIBE by entering your email address

RECEIVE free and discounted e-book offers and inspiring articles delivered to your inbox every week!

Unsubscribe at any time.

SUBSCRIBE NOW!

LOVE TO READ CLUB

visit **LOVETOREADCLUB.COM** ▶

CPSIA information can be obtained
at www.ICGtesting.com
Printed in the USA
LVOW05*2033060817
544058LV00018B/236/P